CORP

SURVIVING CUBICLE
WARFARE

FRANK| Cervi

This is a work of fiction. The characters, incidents, and dialogue, except for incidental references to public figures, products, or services, are imaginary and are not intended to refer to any living persons or to disparage any company's products or services.

Also by
Frank Cervi

PRETTY LIES PERISH

UNCLE NICK: DIARY OF A
MISANTHROPE
&
BURNING THE MIDNIGHT

CONTENTS

CORPORATELAND

SURVIVING CUBICLE WARFARE

www.frankcervi.com

BRIEFING

You are about to embark into a world of grand skylines, fancy restaurants, horrible commutes and even worse, people you don't like. My name is Troy McAvoy. Some of you may've heard of me, most of you will have not; that's because I was in the position you're standing in now, long before your father busted force into your beautiful mother. If you're old enough and have been in the Game before, some of you will know me as Troy '8-Ball' McAvoy. That's right, I did a lot of fucking coke during the 1980's, so what? *Everyone* did. I just did it better. I have more experience in one skin cell on my cock than you have around your entire, fuck'n body. That's ok though, this is a place of learning and it's my job to train you for what is to become your daily grind; a grind that has been done by many before you. Many fail and many will want to dive briefcase first into that sea of traffic on the highway, as office commuter's speed towards their cubes in the grand towers that reach the heavens.

That grind is getting harder and less rewarding by the day, as the fabric and soul of America's workplace becomes even more tattered. Your job, as a corporate grunt, is not without its perks, but those luxuries are proving more difficult to acquire due to changes in the economic landscape and other social factors within other institutions of life. It never used to be this stressful; it never was suppose to be this dirty. It was never supposed to be a war out there on the roads and in the break room or behind closed door meetings.

To give you an illustration, let's start with about 300 million people in the United States. Consider that half of them are retired or in school or on welfare. A fourth is taking care of the retired ones and the ones who are still in school. So now you've got roughly 75 million left. However, 29 million people work for the Federal Government which means only 46 million are left to bring home the bacon; or what's left of it after taxes. Ah, but wait. Then there is the 15 million who work for the local governments, so they're only marginally more worthwhile than the Feds. We're now down to 31 million now. 80% of the aforementioned 31 million are lazy, apathetic, and mostly unproductive, or they're busy undoing the damage done by the doofuses every day.

So, really, there are only 6 million people in this country doing real, actual, productive, innovative hard work. Those 6 million people are not only feeding 300 million, but providing them with warm homes in the winter and quality television programming. The comfort food and *Friends* reruns keep the unproductive, roiling masses from rioting. Karl Marx was wrong: Religion is not the opiate of the people, T.V is.

We here at CorporateLand understand your pain. We understand why you're here; because you want to be better than the bums and the lazy parasites that walk around this country, begging for a handout. Ultimately, you will be better and it is alas why you feel the way you do around the majority of people. It explains why, when you are in a room full of twenty people, you feel as though you're the only one getting anything done. Human exploitation and slavery have always existed, and will forever exist in some form as long as the human race is around this gutter ball in outer space. Human stupidity and WILLFUL ignorance are endless natural resources to be exploited.

If not exploited to some productive end, human stupidity would be a massive net loss for society. I have long said this. Most of the human race is ok with their own slavery in one form or another, as long as they feel 'safe'. Most human beings do not like having to think for themselves. They want to pass that responsibility onto others much smarter than them.

That being said, I personally believe that this modern form of voluntary slavery (corporate life): multilevel enslavement, (personal debt, college debt, marriage/divorce debt, etc.), is the best, most humane type of slavery system that has ever existed in human history; by far. Stupid, thoughtless people crave their own slavery, and so they have it. For the small minority that does not want to be enslaved there are clearly other options.

Contrast our current system with other past systems of FORCED slavery, and any rational man should be able to see that this type of system is likely the best we've got. Enjoy it while it lasts. I believe this current system is in full-failure mode and the older system will likely begin to rear its ugly head once again. If it were me I'd take voluntary tours-of-duty in the corporate world any day than being forced into bondage; at least we can teach you here how to control your environment and make the situation less painful than it has to be.

The rub of the beef though is that you will also experience this in the corporate world now. There are many who are lazy and inept at what they do. We here at CorporateLand will teach you how to work smarter, not harder as the Game has changed since the 50's and 60's.

Much has changed since the 1970's, and that is why I am here, as the Head Officer of the *CorporateLand* training facility. This facility was build shortly after the 80's due to the need of a unique re-training program from higher-ups, who saw the void after so many needless and moronic workplace polices had taken hold over Corporate America. Here, everything will seem real; the buildings, the offices that we will train in, the destinations we will travel to, and the people that you will meet during your instruction. However, it's all a simulation. The situations, examples and exercises are all programmed from years of experience in the field; in order to give you the most efficient basic training before you enter the real deal.

With all that said, it's time to begin. Choose from the many suits, ties, shoes and accessories from our armory so that we may blend in with the program and the inhabitants of CorporateLand. Your journey awaits you beyond the grand commute to our destination.

Nailing *the* Interview

LET'S BE REAL HONEST. People, in general, typically tend to get beyond fucking weird in job interviews. I mean the interviewers, mostly. Your interviewers, in CorporateLand, will typically be the ditzy Twenty-Something college grad who has her BA in bullshit and a life-long passion for tyranny and control. They ask weird ass fucking questions, posit bizarre scenarios and attach massive overemphasis to things that even they—the make-work cretin—would never even do in the real world. I've never understood why this phenomenon persists with HR. Perhaps I should've taken more Psych classes. For the last decade we here have noticed a trend in HR through some of the prep courses being taught in schools around the country. One of my colleagues noticed that the prep course years ago were nearly half men and half women—however, the men were always in Labour Relations (negotiating collective agreements) or Occupationally Health and Safety.

But, they've since noticed a shift in the last year or so that the split has changed and in the last two classes they had it contained all women except for one guy in each class (and working in Labour Relations). HR is now effectively becoming another pink-collar ghetto; full of women who haven't taken any of the hard courses so that they could specialize in the hard areas of HR, but instead specialize in the easy stuff (Employee Engagement being one).

What to do before Tailor your resume to the Company. Don't overdo it, but tweak it here and there. That said most people cannot cope with a resume that is not chronological. I have no idea why, but that is the case. **Research the Company.** And do more than just go to their Homepage. Listen to the last few earnings calls, read over the last few months of mission statements/agenda's, and read the last ten questions.

This is of course if you—like we've mentioned earlier— really *give a shit* about the gig, the rules, and are going 'long' on the company. If you just want to pump-and-dump the business, like you should in this day in age, then by all means do the bare minimum to make the cut. All you have to do, to show how much of a bottom-bitch you can be for them, is to make a statement like, *"I listened to the last earnings call, and I was really impressed/blown away/concerned about..."*

Remember, corporations only care about what you can do for them and not what they can do for you; because you're a peon. So, act like one, and you'll be sure to get a call within 5 days saying "you're hired!"

Research the Interviewer (s). As we all know, many people today are easily accessible online, such as on LinkedIn. That's fair game. Don't be a level 5 predatory about it though and make it awkward by discussing what a 'big fan' you are of their daughter's Jr. High volleyball team.

Best Days If for some reason the company gives you the luxury of having any input in when you'd like your interview to take place during the workweek, do everything in your power to AVOID MONDAY's and FRIDAY's. On Monday, everyone is busy, as *fuck*. Usually, everyone has at least three or more standing meetings on a Monday, and the last goddamn thing they want to do is interview some young whipper-snapper; puckered for perfection on this messiest of workdays. The main problem though is that HR sits around with their thumbs up their asses all day, every day, so they don't really think about that sort of shit. You may think Friday's would be a solid time to book your ~~interrogation~~ interview since it's TGIF and everyone should be in a chill and relaxed mood.

However, TGIF is precisely the point as to why this notion would be counterproductive to your interview success. Some managers usually take Friday off and for them to do the commute—just to interview your ass—will already be a huge piss-off for them. Most people on Friday have checked out completely, so it's best to avoid. If you can pick a time, shoot for 10am-2pm. Most companies do all-day interviews, so no need to avoid lunches because they are either bringing it in from a catering company or taking you out to lunch themselves—depending on how prestigious the business.

Clean up your Social Media.

Look, nobody should give a shit about what you do in your spare time, what your political views are, or that you pop bottles and get high on the weekend with your buddies. Your manager isn't going to go looking for that shit. You know who is, though? H-fucking-R. And let me tell you, they're pretty little fucks about it. Since HR has nothing better to do all day, they've become masters and professionals when it comes to digging up dirt on anyone who walks through the company doors. Hell, they'll know if you farted in the elevator on your way up, seriously!

What to Do Before & During the Interview

This should go without saying, but we must cover even the most common of basics, however universal; because I can guarantee there will always be a small percentage of people, who for some reason, lack common *fucking* sense. Show up *15 minutes* before your interview, and for God fuck'n sakes, come prepared. Remember, you live and breathe in the concrete jungle that is CorporateLand. Generally, your commute from the Outer-Rim (aka Suburbia) can be anywhere from 30 min to 1 hr depending on how far you live from the core and how much you will be fucking with traffic that day.

Try to account for weather and traffic/delays. You wouldn't have to do all of this shit if you lived like a normal human being (free and independent), but you're here now and obviously opted to join the machine. Firstly, be polite to the receptionist upon arrival. Most hiring managers are friendly with their front desk and if you are a dick to the sweet old ladies or the young, hot and tight that are at the frontline, you can be sure they'll relay that impression to said hiring manager—especially if she is fucking the hiring manager or involved flirtatiously in any way (We will cover office SEXcapades at another time, don't worry).

When the interview starts, stay calm. Remember, you have to think of the interview like a date or when you are trying to get into the panties of a woman. You are the suitor trying to seduce the company into 'hiring you' for the 'job'. It's a perfect analogy because, really, it's most likely going to be women who are doing the interviewing (i.e. most HR personnel are women). Yes, you do have to impress the hiring manager (who will most likely be a man) but your main obstacle will be the HR ditz. It doesn't matter if she is seasoned or young, both carry a heavy weight when it comes to seduction; your tactics just have to change slightly when trying to impress the Twenty-Something Party-gurl vs. the single-mom or divorced veteran from HR. Just like with women, think 'Abundance Mentality'. Maybe you get the gig, maybe you don't; take your best shot at it, and the outcome is what it is and then move on.

Learn from the experience. It's perfectly fine to bring a leather portfolio. Don't bring a briefcase. You haven't earned it yet. Have at least 3-5 extra copies of your resume with you, as well as a few copies of your reference sheet. It's not likely that anyone will ask or need them, but if they do, you'll look smoother than a Latina's oiled beach bum. Sometimes, Hiring managers get sent to interviews for people they would not otherwise, and they might've not been given your stats, so again, like we've said above; stay calm and come prepared.

Do not have a stupid email address. Huggable-poohnuts@dumbfuck.com is just not a percentage move. This may seem obvious, but believe me, people still come into interviews with their very first MSN Hotmail address, trust me. It just screams lazy, and that you're outdated; Also, an idiot.

When you meet the hiring manager, shake their hand. Your handshake should be firm— but please, Jesus, Christ, DO NOT be one of those guys who feels like he has to try and crush the other dude's hand to show dominance. Keep them dry too. Also, I guess, shake the hand of the HR Party-gurl; even though you might be brought up on sexual harassment charges on the spot, nowadays. It's ok if you have to wipe your hand on your trousers first. Most people would prefer that you do if need be to a clammy handshake that feels as if you've just handled seafood; Three pumps, no more, and then a clean release. Again, do the same with the chick from HR; again, she'll probably throw you in jail later anyway from pumping and dumping her. Try and maintain good eye contact. Not the no-blinking, *"Yes, I'm a total coke fiend"* kind, but the normal, good kind; that says you're not a total fucking nutjob. The biggest misconception that people have is they believe that interviewers constantly monitor your body language.

This is absurd and honestly impossible given all the other shit they have to think about and process whilst talking to you. While they do not overtly look for body language, it will register, subconsciously. So the impression you make with your body language will be residual in nature and will register with a person on a more intuitive, gut-check level. Only accept the offer of water, coffee or whatever if you can drink it without shaking like Michael J. Fox. You don't want your interviewees thinking *"What earthquake?"* while you spill the beverage all over your mouth, convincing them that you do indeed, have a drinking problem, literally.

Now, if you **DO** have cerebral palsy, please make this clear to them, naturally. If you have to use the bathroom, that's ok too. But do try to take care of that stuff beforehand. The worst thing that you could do is leave your interviewers hanging while you go and throw the biggest dump of life; paying tribute to the porcelain God's for 10+ minutes. If you are in an all-day interview, the best time to go would be in-between interview sessions or at lunch of course. Unless you have explosive, ring-of-fire diarrhea, you should probably pack some pink liquid and down that shit, pronto.

The Importance of Having a Wank

I can't stress enough about the importance of clearing the pipes, especially if you work for Wall Street, with numbers, or are constantly around any high-frequency action. Hell, I'll still 'beat-my-bag' even if I have a girl or a nice rotation of them. Sometimes it's not about the sexual; it's about maintenance and clearing the fog out of your head that could lead to distracting thoughts. Sometimes you just got to get the juice out of the prune sack to make the world sane again. I've missed meetings and mornings before. I don't *fuck'n* care. One time, before heading off to work for a *stupid* Team Building Exercise meeting, I was watching the Weather channel. They had this new young chick on—decked out in your standard 'Get ratings' outfit. I mean, this chick had the tightest top and skirt on that it looked as if she was planning on getting fucked at the bar that morning, which I found so erotic I had to stay home, miss the meeting, jerk off twice. Aimless, I spent the whole morning in a daze and spiked my coffee too much thereafter, so I took the rest of the day off and called in sick; blamed it on the weather. Fuck it, right?

Why go into work after *that*? By the time I would have completed my commute, it would've been noon. Then what? Do *maybe* one hour of solid work and then have to head on home again? Waste of time. What would've been the point? If I didn't jerk off all over myself that morning I wouldn't have been productive at work, anyway. I would've been thinking about that ripe weather girl and her fucking tits, with her 'fuck me' hair and her 'come-fuck-me' skirt. I would've had to do a line of coke in the bathroom that day, just to stay sane!

Jacking-off, however, is an open suggestion and personal preference as it could ease the tension and also prevent you from thinking about the **100 ways** you'd like to bang the HR chick in that very office. Do this of course in the comfort of your own home; like the other aforementioned human functions of the body.

Be aware that most interviewers will lead with the question *"Tell me about yourself"* because people have no filters these days and will usually say stuff they shouldn't— which HR loves and salivates over. Don't tell 'em you think jacking-off before work comes highly recommend, by you—and that it's a tool for consummate professionalism.

Some other quick Tips:

Be Honest. If you lie, your hiring manager will figure it out. If not, HR will. It will sink you, even if they otherwise would've hired you.

Be Concise. Your hiring manager is on the right side of the desk to tell long stories about the hills of Ireland and the days of yore; where they seem to lose the point, but then tie it all up with a nice ribbon and a bow at the end. You're not. Don't be abrupt, but don't make them lose the plot and then have to go hunting for it like Elmer Fud.

Have Examples. If you tell your hiring manager you're awesome, they'll want you to prove it to them. If they ask you to walk them through your resume, be able to do it and also tell them some skills/anecdotes that aren't on your resume, but are relevant.

Show that you're Employable. One of the best ways you can do this is by telling your interviewers how you would go about doing the job you're being interviewed for. It's rare that a candidate does this even though you might think otherwise. Usually, people are more passive. When you're more experienced, you can lay this Awesomeness Grenade down: *"Let me tell you how I would do this job. I've done [all/part/something similar to] it before. My skills are portable."* If you get it right, it's a total win on the battlefield of interviews and you will be sure to blow off your hiring manager's toupee and the HR babe's panties. She'll suggest hiring you to her manager just because you gave her the 'tingles' from pulling the pin on that grenade and showing spine/leadership.

You didn't brag, you lead by example vs. bragging idiotically about how you were a part of a fraternity in college, and can crush 12 beers in an hour while benching 240 lbs.

It's good to remember though that people tend to get massive OCD about shit people say in interviews, so you may need to couch it in terms of ascertaining the firm's or institution's risk tolerance/corporate culture.

What to do after the Interview:

Unclench, it's over. You can relax now; you just seduced and mind-fucked the HR chick as well as your hiring manager, bravo. Have a cigarette, but don't; because smoking is a sign of weakness and a tendency towards the self-destructive. Have a mental cigarette, instead. After you send a "Thank you" letter/email to everyone you interviewed with, you can print them up, but try to change the middle paragraph at least to make them seem more organic.

Paragraph 1: "Thank you for the opportunity to interview with Hammersmith & Goldshits/Perfect Pussy Gentlemen's Club/JesusSaves Credit Union..."
Paragraph 2: "I thoroughly enjoyed our discussion of the aerodynamic nature of Sophia' Vergara's tit's, and whether or not your HR assistant does threesomes on the weekend."

Paragraph 3: *"I think I can be an asset to your firm because... I am a desperate fuck that needs a job in this shitbox of an economy because I foolishly knocked up my girlfriend and now she wants a house in the burbs; plus she'll probably divorce me in 5 years after I get a promotion."*

Something along those lines...

Questions: Like Gun's, they should be *Treated as if they're Loaded*

Tell me about yourself. As we've gone over, this will be asked as an opener because people suffer from verbal diarrhea when asked to talk about themselves as if they were Leonardo Dicaprio on Ellen. Hiring managers especially ask this question first, if they are coming into the interview cold, which happens sometimes.

What do you know about our Company? They don't really give a shit about what you know about their company. This is equivalent to a shit-test that women will give you when first getting to know you. It's not even difficult. Just visit the *fucking* website. Today you can literally do this in the lobby on your phone before the interview if you must. That said, if you haven't, they'll know to ding you because you're either stupid or lazy, or both. Research earning calls, Quarterly Reports and Blog posts if it calls for it. That will impress the fuck-me-Jesus out of them.

Why should I hire you? Being able to count off a bunch of reasons with relevant examples is a Goddamn, fucking home run [We'll cover this further].

Tell me a joke. This question/statement does happen to come about, believe it or not. It's a curveball designed to see how you'd handle weirdness, apparently. Don't ask me why they pose this; ask HR who comes up with these stupid, fucking, psycho-analytical questions. Obviously just tell a simple, modest joke. It doesn't matter. Just don't tell the real funny ones [i.e sexist, racist, bigoted jokes]. You know... the jokes that make comedy what it is.

Do you want the Job? This is another "old guard" question. They're trying to see if you will betray a lack of commitment by equivocating.

Tell me about how you manage projects/time. Maybe you have a better way of doing it than your manager does. They keep a work list. Just show them you can manage time and are not a complete fuckhead. For "problem-solving questions", think out loud. These sorts of 'left field' questions ("Fermi problems") sometimes come up. *"How many dogs are there in the United States?"* Who the *fuck* knows and cares, right? And how is it relevant? HR doesn't give a shit what you think, remember?!

But rather than thinking for 45 seconds and blurting out an answer, say something like, *"Well the population is ~300 million, and let's assume 3 people per household on average. That's 100 million households and let's assumes 40% of those households have dogs. So there are 40 million dogs. But some dog owners have more than one dog, so let's say 1.8 dogs per household, which gives a figure of 72 million dogs."* I just came up with that now and did that all in my head. They don't really care about the actual answer as *nobody* fucking knows the exact number!

All they want to see from you is problem-solving and how you **logically** came to a conclusion using Grade 8 math and a bit of creativity. **What is your biggest weakness?** Fuck, really? Do people still ask this question anymore? Come on! Whatever you say, don't answer with *"I'm a perfectionist,"* *"Honesty"* (especially if it's a bank/brokerage firm), or *"Redheads/blondes"*; unless you really don't give a shit about the interview and just want to fuck around at that point. If it's just you and another guy and no HR bitch, then "Redheads" can be pulled off and be hilarious, but it's still dangerous in this particular PC culture we find ourselves in today. You really don't know if your hiring manager is a real man, or some limp-wristed, salmon jeans wearing mangina behind a desk (closet SJW).

So how do you answer? Well, lead with strength, and then discuss a weakness. For example, you're a 'deal' kind of guy. You're good at building rapport, and also very good at getting people to do what you want them to do in negotiations. You know what you suck at? Regulatory bullshit.

You, my friend, would rather watch old people fuck like two ham sandwiches slapping together, stay at home chewing aluminum foil or masturbate with sandpaper whilst learning the metric system, than deal with regulations. In all seriousness, here is what you'd actually say, *"I'm a deal guy. I'm very good at getting to agreements. I need to improve on the regulatory side of things. I view the opportunity here as a chance to do this because...XY & Z."* You can say this, and make it sound believable, because it's true. Usually, anywhere you work is going to have a Compliance Department, so all you have to do once you get the job is to be smart enough to spot an issue, and walk it the fuck over to them. When you are working for a company, try to set the land speed record for walking said shit over to them. This is not because you give a shit— because a lot of regulations are total bullshit— but because you don't want it to be YOUR problem. It's all about covering your ass and not be liable. The FCPA or the UK Bribery Act (Or wherever you're from) are both stupid and overreaching, but you know what? *Violating* them can get you jail time, and you should be allergic to prison; so comply like a good little motherfucker and then go back to making deals like a boss.

And let's not get started on FATCA, which should be called "FUCKYA" since that's what it's all about—fucking you over.

If you want to be a Total Dickhead

I hate HR as much as any other sane person. I truly believe that Human Resources is literally one of the biggest threats (bigger than terrorism, gonorrhea, and 'selfie' culture combined) to future economic growth, the American way of life and in short, Western civilization. It rules with an iron fist over a vital bottleneck of the economy (the labor market) and is manned by ineffectual, incompetent bitter people whose primary motivation is NOT choosing the best people, but derive a high-functioning orgasm from wielding power over others. However, even though HR and their bureaucratic minions may seem to portend ill for you and I—and pretty much anyone who passed calculus in high school—, there are ways to circumvent HR because they are, after all, some of the dumbest people on earth.

Here in CoporateLand, we can have fun with them and answer to them in some *awesome* ways. In the real world you can answer their standard/popular questions like this if you really *don't* give-a-shit about the job or just want to be the dickhead.

When they ask the question **"Where do you see yourself in 5 years"**, you can reply with something like the following:

Answer—*"Not here because CorporateLand is so unreliable in terms of long term sustenance that I presume I will be working for your competitors or collecting a welfare check because you (HR) have made it impossible to work anywhere and maintain sanity."* Or perhaps, *"I'm so glad you asked! Allow me to bore you for several minutes with a mountain of overly-cheerful and optimistic BS about my future. I'll either be happily working for you OR winning a Nobel Prize for getting kola bears to hump more. Either way, my future is brighter than a pair of albino asses bathed in sunlight!"*

"Have you ever had a disagreement with your boss, how did you handle it?"

Answer— *"Of course, I had another baby boomer boss ask me to put together a PowerPoint or an MS Excel spreadsheet because he 'didn't have time to learn Excel. I said 'O.K,' pay me all of your social security I've given you old timer and we'll chat."*

"Why do you want to work here?"

Answer—*"Let me rephrase that question for you * Please spend the next few minutes complimenting me and gargling my company balls."*

"What's your greatest weakness?"

Answer—*"I can answer this one of two ways: I can take the honest, humble route and actually tell you a weakness. OR, I can just spew some putrid filth about how my greatest weakness is actually some sort of strength. Either way, the point of this question is to get me to admit fault and look weak in front of you so that you can jack/jill yourself off later tonight knowing you crushed my soul. So why not just skip the question and I'll just get naked and you can beat me with a sack of turnips for few minutes? It's basically accomplishing the same thing."*

"Tell me about yourself"

Answer—*"Oh boy an open-minded question, eh?...This is like asking me to slow dance to the sound of hyenas mauling the eyes out of a gazelle. There is going to be no rhythm to my answer. Just erratic snapping sounds mixed with an occasional whimper."*

Of course, there is another alternative, an extreme maybe: Simply refuse to be interviewed by HR. I know I am just waxing philosophical right now, but here me out. You see, no matter what the unemployment rate is, companies and corporations still **need** employees. No matter how bad it gets out there, they still need us as much as we need them for jobs. Most people don't realize this and go and totally short-sell themselves, looking at a 9% unemployment rate.

But what if, just what *fuck'n* if, people were sick and tired with the pretentions, pee pickers, and arrogant morons in the HR department and simply refused to interview with *them*? What if some sort of grass roots movement involving job seekers, graduates, and the future life-blood of corporations, all of a sudden got an ounce of self-respect and said, *"Eh! You know something, I'm no longer interviewing with HR. If you want to consider me for a genuine position within your company, then you have me talk to the hiring manager or boss of that position. Not some idiotic 23 year-old HR ditz who graduated 2 weeks ago, doesn't know jack-fuck about my job, let alone the industry."* Ask yourself this; "Have you ever gotten a job through HR?" Didn't think so. There is no reason for them to be involved in the hiring process. There never was before. Now you can see that there is no downside to this type of refusal. Nobody gets a job through HR.

They offer NOTHING to the potential candidate, the potential talent, the potential future leader and innovator. It's like having the popular high school chick or "prom queen" threaten she'll never go out with you or suck your dick—she would never go out with you in the first place, ergo the threat is a hollow one; much like her head. Anyways, back to reality and some advice that will help you since HR will unfortunately be in attendance in the real world.

Questions you should ask your Interviewers

Why should you hire me? Remember above how we said we'd come back to this one? If your hiring manager hadn't already asked you the reversal of this, then this would be a perfect time to do so. The more reasons you can count off, the better they will like it. Done correctly, it's a show-stopper. Champagne and strippers type show-stopper.

What you will close with: *"Based on our discussion today, is there anything about my candidacy that you perceive as a weakness? Is there anything I can provide a fuller discussion of?"*

Here's why these types of questions are so powerful in your arsenal for interview mission success. Either a) there's nothing they perceive as a weakness in which case they hear themselves say that (aka Reverse Psy-ops), or b) there is something and you get a chance now to address it and get your side of the story out. Q: ***"Tell me why you withdrew for two semesters."*** A: *"I decided to travel to Australia in order to bang beautiful women instead of the dyke-cut, cottage-cheese dimpled sows, here."*

Or, *"My father died and I had to go run a business for a year, just like Jimmy Stewart in 'It's a wonderful Life'. The board voted down Mr. Button-down MintGreen, but only if I stayed and ran the Building & Loan dept."* Pick the latter if you want the job and the former if you're just yanking their chain for a laugh.

Secrets of the Temple

They *will* talk about you. If you show, in any attackable way, that you are a fucking weirdo—bad B.O., picked your schnauzer in front of them, or eye-fucked the shit outta the HR blonde; i.e. broadcasted jerk-off fantasies through your facial antenna towards her subconscious (she will know)— it will be discussed.

So best behavior, and use your indoor voice. Sometimes they TRY to hire women. There is all this bullshit out there about how corporations are still somehow of the "patriarchy" and if anything, just hire women who are hot, with fake tits. And by "Try" I mean on a 'straight-up' basis— no gimmicks, affirmative-action, or pressure from governments. The ugly truth is, however, that those women manage to fuck-up the interviews at alarming rates. When corporations DO find a female candidate that they'd like to make an offer to, they [the female candidates] can't make up their fucking minds.

This happens no matter what. The woman can literally be the last person in her department at a company that had just filed for bankruptcy and still not take the offer. I've heard of instance where a woman being considered for a job asked the company to keep the job open for her for six months. Six months? It's understandable if you have a couple other interviews you're going on. But Six, Fucking, Months? Sorry Princess Starbucks, they're not going to hold the job for you while you shop for a better offer. Typical is such hubris. Oh, and you know who is hardest on other female candidates? HR of course: HR is filled to the brim with women who'd love to stick it to Princess Starbucks.

So inconsiderate, I mean, they don't even think of the effect their hubris has on the poor male hiring-manager who has to put up with hearing all the HR chicks going off about a woman's choice in shoes for the interview; like he would possibly give a shit. Women fail in these areas because they treat interviews like they treat dating—as if *they* are being courted when in fact it's always the candidate who is trying to seduce the company. That's why men are better at it. It's our game. It's not a situation where playing 'hard-to-get' will net you benefits unless you, as a candidate, are in high demand. Which we can all safely assume, most aren't. Most candidates for jobs are desperate and are at the very bottom of desirability when it comes to hiring.

They only care about two things: First, can you do the fucking job they want you to do, or are they going to have to continuously correct your stupid mistakes? Second, are you going to be a team player or a whiny fucking bitch (Another reason why more women don't get hired)? They don't need you to be best buds, but they *do* need to be able to count on you to do your job, and not be a fucknut. Real hiring Managers (men) go with their gut. Their instincts are finely tuned. They trust them. That's why they are managers. Their armor bears the scars of many an internecine war, and they are goddamn fucking survivors. They are the Honey badger of CorporateLand, only without the fagotty fuck'n British guy from BBC doing a voiceover of their daily activities.

An example would be a hiring manager being the only person out of 12 to ding a guy. For whatever reason, he doesn't like him. The candidate could seem nice enough, but there's just something about him. For whatever reason, the head of HR wants to plow the road for him and the company hires said 'nice guy'. Four months later the company has to fire said 'nice guy' for trying to punch out two vice presidents at a party (Don't worry, we will talk about Office Party's later). This scenario seems extreme, but shit like this does happen and a hiring manager's instincts should always take a front row eat over some HR chick's panty-tingles. That is why if corporations want to hire the best and stay as productive as possible, HR should be eliminated as an entity entirely from the corporate world.

Sadly, HR, and their destructive PC/fem-centric policies are the reasons why CorporateLand is in decline and why men (who are able to) are opting out en mass. If you are an SJW, they (real male managers) will NEVER HIRE YOU. If you are applying to a more female-dominated institution or company, then this issue does not apply to you; for you will be among the clergy. For men seeking a tolerable CorporateLand (one that is waning), the last thing a hiring manager wants to listen to is some twat drone on about his/her political views. Most of these corporations today always have some of these interns and twats milling about that they can barely stand.

They [The PC folk] all have this idea that they are entitled to be included in every fucking conversation known to man and that everyone should gape in the wonder of their stupid ideas. This is why any good hiring manager loves it when they see "Gender Studies" or "Oppression Studies" degrees on the top of your resume. They are Giant, Fucking, Red Flags. Signs that say, "Please, don't hire me! I'm a fucking loser!" and "If you hire me, I will be sure to activate a Class Action Lawsuit on this company the day one of my male co-workers stares at me too long." Hiring managers don't care if you are double Ivy with an M.A in Swedish Lesbian Poetry. If they get the slightest whiff that you are an SJW who's going to cause problems, they ding you. They will find a way to do it surreptitiously if they have to, but you will never darken their door again.

Happily, though, SJW's have stupid worthless degrees and experience that is, for the most part, off-point for CorporateLand, so they will rarely get an interview. They are more likely to sue a firm or institution because they got their widdle feewings hurt somehow because they overheard guys talking about slamming pussy on the weekend, or they never got promoted due to sucking hard at life, and their job that they were hired for.

Rules for Shaking a Female Interviewers hand.

Grab her by the pussy. Just kidding! This is an 'old school' rule, and most modern female businesswomen aren't going to mind, however, keep in mind that it's best if you wait for the woman to extend her hand first. Why? Back in the old days of covered wagons, or at least back before colored TV, the thought was that if you offered your hand to a lady to shake, she might not want to shake your hand. That would put her in an uncomfortable position of either an unwanted touch—women were previously thought to be delicate flowers, during both the Victorian Era and Regan Era's—or of refusing, and looking like a cunt and/or embarrassing you, thus embarrassing herself.

That's women, though, basket-cases. So it's best just to wait to avoid all of this over-thinking bullshit that women do in their head all day long. When she puts her hand out, try to clue into whether or not she's offering the dainty-lady shake (palm parallel to the floor and gently take her fingers) or the standard 'man-shake'. Save the cave-manning for the bars.

Entering *the* Rat-Race

CONGRATULATIONS, PRIVATE. You've been hired and passed the interview with flying ribbons of who-gives-a-fuck. Now you will be put to the grindstone as the concrete jungle aims to destroy your soul and your moral compass. You need not fear, as there are tips and ways to remedy this plight; this unsavory human existence that millions of people have to go through day in and day out. You are now the days bitch, you own nothing. You don't own your house, your car, or your life because you don't get to enjoy any of that since you now have to be at a job in order to 'have' those things. You can look, but you can't play or touch. Your time is now the companies. How ironic! By now, you've learned the fundamental lesson that time is *valuable*.

You can't do it all; no matter how many episodes of *Suites* you've watched. Everything you do should be done in conjunction with reflection on whether or not it is a good use of your time. This must become second nature if it hasn't already, I'd suggest getting a journal to organized and record everything. Also, a calendar to write on with erasable markers which show a month or two is very useful.

Find a Mentor/Ally

The first thing you ought to do is find a medium-senior employee who is on top of their shit, relatively approachable, and generally a decent man all around. This man, ideally, will turn into a mentor, officially or otherwise. It is absolutely imperative you find these people if you are in CorporateLand for the long haul. Like we've said before, you are either in CorporateLand for good, or are just here to pump-and-dump it like a Bangkok hooker on a Sunday morning. If you are pumping-and-dumping it would be a waste of your time to seek out a mentor since you'll be happy with an average salary, minimal responsibility, and dropping out of the rat-race once you have leverage and a ton of 'fuck-you money'. Your ally must be a man as well. This isn't a 'sexist' remark.

I'm being serious, as any man should. Do *not* make this mistake and I will tell you why beyond the obvious—workplace dynamics between men and women differ substantially and substantively. Men are in competition with *other* men and women are in competition with *other* women. There are several reasons for this phenomenon but just suffice it to say that men prefer high financial benefits in their work, while women prefer more flexible working conditions—hence, why the vast majority of women **earn** less than men. If you want to succeed, you better be ready to go for the former.

You want a bonus and promotion, not an extra week's vacation, which comes in time. You can't think impulsively and short-term like women do, you have to think of the big picture. Sure, an extra week's paid vacation sounds well and good. However, if you work just a little harder in the SHORT TERM, you'll be making more money in the LONG TERM and will be able to take whatever fucking time off you want, because you will get promoted to a BeefBus position.

While Janice took the low-hanging fruit for a short-term gain instead of thinking long-term, she will be stuck in CorporateLand forever—or until she gets 3x maternity leave, and then quits her job for a bonus spin at life! Benefits of a male mentor include giving you the lay of the land, internal gossip (the useful male kind, not the bullshit about Kelly's toe fungus issue), and a source for real advice.

However, watch who you blow off steam to/or with. I would advise refraining from said action entirely, but some people can't help themselves; as work is stressful and you may want to vent to a co-worker about how you want to murder Kevin in Accounting with a Swingline stapler, for fucking up those files. Or, how you'd want take a hot, steamy shit in Kimberly's coffee mug since she keeps asking you to donate to her kid's sports teams and school trips. Remember, your friends are not in this world, and they will not be able to relate to you when you want to rant about that bitch who stole a file from you when your back was turned. Don't sweat the small stuff, just think of why you are there—to fuck the corporation for a paycheck and get the hell out. You're a whore for them. With that said.

Be a Rock, Mind your Reputation

For some odd fuck'n reason, popular culture has turned where a backstabbing power-broker who slits a few throats along the way is idolized; *House of Cards* maybe? Or, what about the feminization of office culture, perhaps? Backstabbing is a predominantly feminine trait, so I will go with the latter of those two. Mark my words— your reputation is worth far more than your paycheque.

The world of CorporateLand is a lot smaller than you think and it loves gossip because, frankly, there is nothing better to do; and the work itself is pretty boring most of the time. Being a *rock* is what you want to be. Your office should be 'Patrick Bateman' immaculate. Keep your door open (if you have one), and every time someone comes in you'll look on top of shit, and not stressed. This optic is enormously important. Your role in the office is the *role-model*. You're probably thinking *"Why the fuck do I want to be the 'role-model' when all I want is to fuck the company, get my money, and go?"* Being the *role-model* means that other interns (particularly women) will come to *you* to blow off steam, gossip, complain, ask for advice, etc. DO NOT backstab these people, and keep your word. You're their "rock" and you want them to gossip about you in this way, not in the way they gossip about Beth's "incident" at the company's Christmas party[Side note: Try not to go to office party's. We will cover this in another protocol, so don't worry].

Having this will make your office life a whole lot smoother, and all you have to do is tiddy the fuck up every now and then, dress nice, and not look like a divorced twice, beaten dog— who looks as if he's ready to go 'Postal' when walking in from the parking lot. You don't have to even say much, just listen and add little injections her and there empathetically. You're not here to Game or fuck the women at the office so you feel free to go half beta/Alpha with regards to interaction. Again, you don't want to be a total pussy, but at the same time, you don't want to be a total dick. So fake it.

Benefits of being the *role-model* will include you being able to learn everyone's secrets without them knowing yours. You will also learn where they stand vis-a-vis their competition with you. You will be respected by your peers, and if you're good to your reputation, which is worth your weight in gold, it will pay dividends later on. The neckbeard who is a mess that came to you for advice could very well become the next Zuckerberg when he realizes that this [cubicle life] wasn't for him. You want to be there down the road when he has a business to transact, a lucrative job to offer, or a summer place in Italy you can stay at for free.

Keep your Priorities

As you know, your time is valuable and it's just about to get even more valuable. I say this in a qualitative way—you will likely be able to actually calculate your time, whether it's by the hour or otherwise. But also, in a qualitative way—you're simply going to have less of it.

When you're going to the office for 7:30 am and leaving routinely past 6pm or longer, it's less and it takes getting use to. This grind and inhumane treatment of your mental and physical states will help you realize what *time* actually is, and how you value it. You can actually calculate the value of your time on a personal level with work by reference to your hourly rate, taking into account the marginal value of personal time.

Here are some tips:

a) Keep lifting, boxing, running, whatever your dig is. It's hard to fit it in, I know, but you need to think about it in weeks not days. You will need to have the flexibility to stay late on any given day. However, you will need a back-up plan to make up for that some time later in the week.
b) DO NOT PICK UP BAD HABITS. I am looking directly at you—alcohol, cigarettes, and bad food. You're probably thinking *"Oh, so you mean no fun!"* I'm saying to you that you won't be much of a Playboy, whose slay'n after hours at the bars, when you have the body that most 35+ office stooges possess these days in CorporateLand.

You know who I'm talking about, right? I am talking about Jerry in Accounts Receivables; who looks like the spawn of a manatee, who had sex with an orangutan. Or, how about Bill in the marketing department; who looks akin to the Michelin Man without his suit jacket on? Do *you* want to be like Jerry and Bill, who's highlight of their day is to have jacked-off in the shower because their wives are now fucking the Denny`s waiter who CAN actually see his own dick in the morning? No, that doesn`t sound negotiable now, does it? You want to be ready when you're done work to go and slay pussy; the young, tight and hot gazelles at the bar later, or if you`re married, at least still be able to give your wife the tingles she needs to consider hoping on 'pop' for bit after your Netflix session.

Just because everyone else is going for a smoke, doesn't mean you need to so as well. In addition, many of these office types have "traditions" or rituals that they oddly abide by with no reason whatsoever aside from said rituals getting them through the day, or creating commonality. These traditions can vary but usually its coffee runs to Starbucks or Tim Horton's or drinking at the first floor bar on Friday evenings, or something along these lines of interference. Since you are new and trying to make an impression (to be seen or of the group), you will feel somehow compelled or even obligated to attend events or partake in the fetching of coffee. If one of these traditions crosses your path in Corporateland culture and are not mandatory then DO NOT feel obligated to partake. Following is for the weak and dependent. Plus, buying coffee for you and other co-workers a few times a week or everyday can seriously eat into your wallet. It's unnecessary when you can just brew a batch at work; or bring your own from home like a fucking, fiscally sane person.

If you work at some sort of business firm then it would be ironic for you to waste your money needlessly. Remember, you want to sock away as much of your paycheck as possible so that you don't have to put up with this bullshit for much longer in your life. If you don't have the balls to say NO or still feel insecure that your co-workers may see you as some sort of anti-social recluse then you *aren't* getting it! These people *aren't* your friends; they are people you *work* with.

If you must though, the one thing you can do is make an appearance as often as 'auntie flow' likes to visit Bethany in HR—which turns her into a raging wildebeest.

Show up to casual Fridays once a month if you feel *so* compelled to not be viewed as a wet-blanket or party-pooper. Again, it all depends on what Game or strategy you are running with during your stay in CorporateLand (Long haul or Short run) and what role you are choosing to play (*Role-Model, Office Buffoon, The Fun Intern etc.*). People, in all honesty, don't care as much as you think and the best escape is to just leave. If your work-friend, work-wife, or whomever comes up to you and asks *"Are you going to that thing later tonight, with everyone from the office?"* just don't be there. Plan B is to also have something real scheduled in advance, and be sure to make it healthy and awesome like, *"I have my MMA class tonight."* Or *"I'm playing pick up later at the rink, so I can't."* You're own traditions are healthy, so avoid all of the unhealthy CorporateLand traditions. That is why you're body doesn't and won't look like the rest of your co-workers who needed a Triple By-pass, yesterday.

Benefits of doing this include: Being looked up to for maintaining your health, keeping your own mental sanity in a sea of dysfunction (mental health is a very slippery-slop in this world, do it for this reason if nothing else), and not being there all of the time like a leech; because you're doing cool shit all of the time versus your boring co-workers is seen a positive attribute. You look like less of a loser.

Make "Friends" with HR

Yes, I am going to say this—as much as it makes me hurl to even suggest such a tactic— but you need to make friends with HR. This, in my personal opinion, will be the hardest thing you'll ever have to pull-off in this world, due to principle alone. It doesn't have to be *real*, just make it happen. Treat it like the friendship you'd make with the neighborhood drunk; you make nice since you don't know when or if they will attack you. HR is the Elephants Graveyard for people with no fucking talent. However, there is, inevitably, one person (and usually only one) who does have their head on their shoulder and not completely up their own asshole. So congrats to her (and it's always 'her'). Buddy up with 'her' and make sure she handles all of your HR needs because otherwise, whatever you need done will always get fucked up beyond recognition by girls and/or AA hires who are just there for the numbers and cushy do-nothings. The last thing these sloths want to do is work. All they (the rest of the talentless college-grads) want to do is enjoy their 9-to-5 coffin, collect their paychecks and go home. Sure, there are loads of talented women milling about in CorporateLand...but you won't find them in HR. Understand this, recognize this, and make friends anyways for the greater good of your sanity.

Make Friends with IT

Actually make friends with these guys in the work sense of the term of course. IT sees you when you are sleeping and knows when you're awake looking at porn during lunch. The Eye in the Sky doesn't lie. They know what sites you visit etc. Thus, you need to be a true believer in the separation of Work and State. Your work laptop history (and I mean that thing that *can't* be erased by 'private' browsing or incognito search) should have entirely mundane shit on it; like the lives of most of your co-workers. You need to be mundane and boring, or *appear* to be at least. You need go total suburbanite-commuter, soccer-mom type boring on your laptop. Sites you visit should be work-related (research, travel, etc.). Don't use the company WiFi for your personal devices, either. Keep two mobile phones: work and personal. The joke around the office should be that it's your "Bat phone" and you're Adam West.

This is exactly what Tiger Woods should've had. If he'd had a second phone that was a) Identical to whatever phone his caddy/major domo/little helper dude had and b) HAD A GODDAMN PASSWORD ON IT, he wouldn't have had his wife trying to swing for the 300-yard marker down his driveway at him with one of his Nike clubs. Stupid, stupid, stupid!

When his wife found it he could've said, *"Oh, that's [name of sidekick's] phone. I'll take that and return it to him; thanks sugar-tit's (kisses her on cheek)."* Tiger would've gotten busted eventually, in my opinion, because he was probably fucking half the pussy in America. It was only a matter of time before one of those seasoned whores said something or he was caught in the act. With a second phone though, and a fucking password on it, he would have gotten in at least ten more 'fresh bangs' before his wife came swinging down the driveway like a 10 year-old at a driving range.

You might need a friend in IT someday. IT is never going to land a $20 million contract or account with a new client. They are like the CIA; you only hear about their failures.

Don't Flip a Guy for no Reason

As you can gather, you are most likely going to be working with some people you're just not going to like, maybe even hate. Maybe someone is just having a bad day, its CorporateLand for Christ sakes; someone is always having a horrible day. Its scratch and claw for a dime, so a lot is on the line in terms of survival: Surviving in the terms of your co-worker needing that big promotion in order to pay off the mortgage to his McMansion or to feed the crumb-crunchers at home because the wife quit her job for the fourth time. Maybe Karen is on the rag again.

Who knows, really? The point is, the triggers could be anything for these people; mostly financial in nature and or relationship issues. People can't help themselves when it comes to making bad decisions and overly extending themselves fiscally and emotionally. You need to be a rock, solid. You need to have your *shit together* and not waver when a breeze or typhoon hits your shores at the office. Hurricane Karen may be on your ass about those stupid reports or Suicidal Steve may be depressing the shit out of you in the restroom, with his divorce proceedings, while you're trying to take a massive dump. *You* don't have any of these problems though because *you* don't fuck up like everyone else, right? You have your priorities. You have yourself. Equanimity should be a rule for noobs. Don't let yourself get pushed around or be an emotional punching bag for someone, yet still realize that you will not always have the whip hand in the situation.

Some guy may stiff you on a referral fee. It may have been two grand or more, and he screws you on it. You reach out to him, but he doesn't respond. So, you pick your battles. Not only will this guy never get another referral from you but you manage to drive a few hundred thousand away from his firm. Fight like a ninja in CorporateLand, fight with money. Never go and physically assault someone like this (unless they deserve it). Hurt him where it will really hurt, his wallet or in this case, his firms wallet; which will likely affect his own.

Once you leave CorporateLand, do what you want. Beat him at a bar, slash his tires, fuck his wife, and fuck his mistress and then his wife, fuck both his wife and his mistress at the same time; fuck his daughter who's in college as a cherry on top. Pop her 'cherry' too for bonus points if applicable—then send him a note about you doing said fucking, with panties in the envelope as evidence.

What I'm trying to say is that sometimes, it pays to acknowledge the elephant in the room. Sometimes, it is best to let the elephant starve itself to death because it is in said room [captivity] and not in the wild. For example, you might be working with a salesman, who can't sell, but what he can do is blame other people (you mainly) for his failures. And one day you come out of your office and there he is, coming down the hallway toward you, *"Great,"* you think, *"This asshole."* So you say to him, *"Jimmy, the thing I like about you, and it's the ONLY thing I like about you, is that it pisses you off MORE to see me coming than it does me to see you coming."* Inexplicably, you both will get along just fine after this; you both being men and can maybe laugh about your distain for each other. However, the elephant at the end of the day will starve. He will still be, and always will be, a shitty fuck'n salesman. You win, because you let nature take its course instead of wasting energy and time addressing fate.

Hide in Plain Sight

It's sort of like being the 'Gray Man'. Do you job, get paid, and enjoy your life outside of CorporateLand during your stay here. You have to understand that nobody in CorporateLand is working here because it's so 'fucking cool' and awesome, not even the folks over at Google (Ok fine, maybe Google, but not 99% of the rest.) You and everyone else are here for one thing and one thing only: a paycheque.

Secure the Perimeter. Whether it is business or personal, try to make sure that nobody can come to your boss with a sneak attack or an element of surprise. If anyone asks your boss a question about you, it's better for him to know the answer because it came from *you* first. This way the information presented to him is controlled and always from the source: you. The Information War in the office is just as important to win as the psychological and physical battles you will be facing day in and day out in the trenches.

Don't get overdrawn at the Favor Bank.

There will be times during you tour-of-duty when you will need a friend or for someone to cover your ass.

It's ok to do favors for people, to take on a project or two, because someday...you will need a friend.

Covering another person's region after they've moved on and keeping everything a float is notable.

Most likely, you will work for a firm or corporation that doesn't commensurate with the work you will do, but you can regard this extra work a 'sweat equity'. A good reputation is a powerful shield. Take on extra tasks and projects that you can handle and aren't too demanding. Your goal here is to not overextend yourself and not be a bitch. It's a 'power move' to make yourself look like the shit and a hero so when you need an ally no one will hesitate to be in your corner when the shit-hits-the-fan or you need a favor...like when you eventually make your exit from CorporateLand—whether you give a 2-weeks' notice or just vanish completely.

Containment. Contain your enemies, as George Kennan advised in the Long Telegram. Do no escalate into a hot war if at all possible, while not suffering any loss of prestige. For example, at your job you might have an issue with a female co-worker. The scenario could be that you do not want to do her work for her and she needs you to, because she isn't very good at it. She may also complain that she "has kids" and can't stay late to do it (very common excuse with these types). You of course, being a man, value your free time. Also, your name is not Rumple-Fucking-Stiltskin, and it's not your job to stay late if you don't have to, for no extra pay, to do some incompetent skirt's work because she got promoted into a job she lacked the talent for (also very common).

This tends to happen a lot with the women around the office because some male manager either has the hot's for one, or is *trying* to fuck her or *has* fucked her; and now needs to 'pay' her in some way or to move her office or work closer to said manager's area. We also can't forget affirmative action type policies and promoting women for no reason other than 'Vag'! When they *do* get to these positions, they crumble—because their ego's have been bolstered instead of their skill-set, which the latter being obviously more important to do the job.

Now, if someone needs your help and asks for it and has been an ally in past for you, then it is ok for you to do it on a one-off basis as it can be an equal transaction. It can be useful to have a positive balance in the "Favor Bank" instead of just a balanced one. Anyways, let's go back to our scenario and say that said incompetent skirt is now screaming at you and that you *"have to do this"* for her, and you go ahead and tell her, *"Go fuck yourself with a big black African dildo, cunt muffin!"* She now freaks and thusly goes to her boss, who now goes to your boss. What a cunt, right? So, what do you do? Having explained your shit to the boss, make sure you tell the story of how she tries to dump all of her work on you because she can't do it, and how you solved a bunch of shit because it's easy for you and that you are willing to take one for the team once and a while—but you won't be someone's bitch because she has a vagina and feels entitled.

Something along those lines will do. If your boss is a real man he will understand where you are coming from and also understand how women behave in the workplace and how they try to survive through passivity and manipulation of weaker men. What happens if she is still yapping about it and stamping her feet like the child she is?

Two things: First, go to HR. Remember how we talked about becoming "Friends" with HR, well; this is one of those times where that can pay off. Cultivate the Powers That Be in HR and you will have a firewall or sorts. You have to understand that if you hate this chick who is dumping her work on you, chances are HR does too (since they are all women). Women secretly despise other women, especially ones who get promotions. HR will also see or sniff out how she got her promotion and whether or not 'strings' were pulled for her. That is the ultimate WIN scenario for you in any HR development; for HR or the HMFIC loving you and hating the chick who is giving you shit at the office. The second thing you might have to do is to start shopping around CorporateLand for another job depending on how heated the scenario is. Remember, they can't fuck with you if you have options. So, find another job and make 50% more than you would if you had stayed put. If you leave, leave with **vengeance**. Let it be known that you're not to be fucked with. Let the other work she tried to dump on you stack up and then give it all back to her on your way out the door.

Keep your exit strategy a surprise so that nobody knows and she arrives one morning with a huge work load on her desk. Office whores love big loads anyways, so fuck her. That brings us to the next point.

Make yourself Indispensable, and then Disappear

Try to become the guy who can basically work from wherever you want and don't have to go into the office anymore—it's a fucking dream and ultimate heaven. Go in though, from time to time, but only to renew connections and to see if they've hired any new talent, by which I mean 22 year-old college grads with tight 22 year-old asses (Side note: Don't shit where you eat, of course[we will cover this at length]).

Remember the 'Sweat Equity' thing we talked about? That helps, a lot. How do you get away with all of this? You have to perform at a high level. You always have to be reachable and have a high skill-set that is unique. Also, your employer has to be of the understanding that he pays you for PERFORMANCE *not* for attendance.

Have a Plan for when 'Shit Hits the Fan' (SHTF)

Always have two escape routes and a bug-out-bag of sorts. Eventually, you are either going to want to move up, move on, or escape CorporateLand completely. Whatever your mission, you need to have a battle plan ready to execute at a moment's notice. Remember, in order to do this successfully and without much friction you have to have personal leverage first and by doing a lot of the things that we've talked about so far can go a long way in securing that leverage in the form of a CorporateLand currency. Money is not important in CorporateLand, in the same way that it is important in ConsumerWorld. In CorporateLand, the currency is your reputation, which can come from 'Sweat Equity' and of course your talent and likeability around the office. However modified or illusory it is, it is still important. None of your persona has to be real, it just has to stick and stick well. If you don't like what you are doing for a living, you can walk away and still make six figures doing what you do on the side, whatever that may be. By leveraging contacts made in CorporateLand you can consult or create your very own business using all that you've learned by maintaining all of the ally's you've kept.

Most people in CorporateLand are not curing cancer. That's fine. Most jobs' here exist to fund a lifestyle for most people. Nobody on their death bad says, *"I wish I'd spent more time at the office."* As the Christians say, be in the world, but not of the world—or something to that nature. Say what you want about religion, but there are some very wise words in the scriptures and in the good book. Indeed, in CorporateLand you will need to have a bible or some sort of personal religion in order to survive. The only reason to work for a corporation is to make a shit-ton of money. I'm being serious, there are no other reasons and if you think there are any moral ones, or some type of other crusade, you are being delusional. If that's not the case for you, then go do something else. Whatever you do though, don't outspend your paycheque; you'll pay for it in the end with more servitude. Save Crowns and Pounds and Farthings. You will need a war chest someday.

Be Loyal...to you.The days of strolling into IBM or GM at age 21 and walking out at 55 with a fat fuck'n pension and a gold watch garnished with hookers and champagne are LONG GONE. It's everyman for himself these days, BUT it need not be 'Lord of the Flies' out here. It's a war, but a war that is multi-prong and takes an array of tactics instead of just brute force. Every article you see online titled *"Gen X and Gen Y Have No Work Ethic"* should be titled *"Gen X and Gen Y Refuse to be Treated like Commodities; Boomers Outraged!"*

Why the Boomers expect loyalty when they offer none is beyond me and anyone with a fucking brain in their head. You should have loyalty in CorporateLand to a) A paycheque and b) Those of your colleagues who have proven themselves worthy of your loyalty. That's it. The asshats in the C-Suite would just as happily fire you if it would make their stock go up half a point. Have Options. Learn a Trade. Be able to do something so you aren't dependant on CorporateLand Paycheques. The modern trend is leaning towards entrepreneurship. One of the difficulties we face as a society is, *"Where are all of the jobs"* and *"Where will the jobs come from."* New jobs can only come from people starting businesses. For the economy to grow and for us to get out of stagnation requires fresh blood in the form of new business. Men need to have a trade or be working on a side hustle. If you have a trade on the side, then you won't go hungry. Sure, technology is disruptive (look at Uber) but nobody in China or India is going to be able to fix your plumbing.

Avoid Debt. This one is a biggy. Debt or any sort of liability; whether I'd be having to support kids, or a wife who loves to rack up credit card debt whilst not contributing anything monetary to the family unit (even though she is capable of at least part-time work), are the main reasons why most are imprisoned in CorporateLand forever—Doomed to serve a life-sentence.

DO NOT become this guy. Only be a provider figure for you. As mentioned above, the days of walking into IBM and leaving with that gold watch are over. Same goes with marriage and women today. The days of winning the bread and *not* having your wife backstab you 50% of the time and initiating said backstabbing (divorce) 75% of the time are over as well. If you want that shit then you have roughly a 90% that you'll be working in CorporateLand for your remaining years—paying for college, lawyers, alimony etc. The last thing you want to do is pile on educational debt in the form of loans to get a BA or whatever. It's a disaster. Millennial's can't afford to buy a home because they're getting ass-raped without lube on tuition and debt service thereon. And the degree's people get now aren't helping the problem either. I mean, Gender Studies? Come, fucking, on, people! I'd rather my daughter be a hooker; at least she'd be giving society something it needs and isn't totally worthless. Women's/Gender studies is just you looking down at your vagina all day saying, *"Yup, I have a vagina all right...there it is!"*

She'd make a shit ton more than any Gender Studies major anyway and would be given value for her pay. You're better off being a waitress for Christ sakes! Don't kid yourself. People who are on the hiring board at any firm or business in CorporatateLand ding you if you have a shitstain degree like that. Women's Studies? Best case scenario is that she is just a lazy bitch. Worst case scenario, she's a lazy cunt who sues the firm for some harassment bullshit or that the boss didn't say "hi" to her on the way in one day and her *feewings* got hurt, whaahh. Fuck that shit.

The Handling *of* Salary Negotiations

ONCE YOU'VE ESTABLISHED YOURSELF in your first job (note: that's 'job' not career. Nobody really has a career anymore these days), you will eventually decide that the time has come to make more money. Or, you are going to decided that the toxic environment at whatever corporation you work for has become too much for the amount of fiscal compensation they are willing to trade for it. Either way, it's time for you to at least test the waters and see if you can jump ship. The best time to find a new gig is obviously while you are employed and have value in the marketplace. When you're unemployed, or have been for quite some time, you might as well have some sort of infectious disease that someone might catch from you; since that is how you will be treated.

Nowadays, the best way to not get *totally* ripped off on salary, once you've outgrown your current position, is to bail. It's that simple. Either take their ~~'merit pay increase'~~ shitty 3% "COLA" [Cost-of-Living-Adjustment] or pack your bags. If they give you something more than a COLA it most likely means that you should have bailed a long time ago. Most people will put up with 'medium shitty' over unknown anything and CorporateLand knows it.

There is always the possibility that you *might* find a company that does not have its head completely up its own collective asshole, but the odds suck on that one. Forward thinking is just not a hot commodity that is rewarded all that often, because of the tyranny of quarterly reporting. Quarterly reporting rewards "Results: Now" and squeezing every bit of ~~value~~ life out if its employees as if they were the play things of Jeffrey Dahmer. Employees, in the eyes of CorporateLand, are what we call "Cost centers". Alright, let's get into the nitty-gritty then on Salary Negotiations now that we've outlined the battlefield and you are ready to play. Here is one Hard and Fast Rule, no matter what anyone tells you:

Never Ever, EVER tell them what you are making now. Are you writing all of this down? Good. Now, repeat that line to yourself a million fucking times so that when you're on a date with one of these companies in the interview process, you keep your fucking leverage.

The same can be applied to an actual date with a woman, but that's another topic and field guide. If you are asked this in an interview, imagine that I am sitting next to you, telling you that I will bash your skull into a chutney pulp with a sledgehammer—until the coroner can only identify you through dental records—if you dare tell the HR lady and hiring manager what you make or made at your previous gig. Then, I will piss on your corpse—while telling your lifeless body that I was right when I said, *"Don't EVER tell them what others valued you at"*.

Whatever 'reason' they give you for 'Needing' to know your Salary History is complete and unqualified, Bullshit.

How so, you ask? First, the motherfuckers sitting across from you have already budgeted for the position and thus, they already know what they're willing to pay for it. So, fuck them; they're just trying to screw you. CorporateLand is just a giant game of who fucks who first in the asshole with the metaphorical shaft. Oh, and it's going to be the people who don't want to tell you what their proposed salary range is that are the most insistent on *you* telling them. Sometimes you will get some sob story about *"managing equity in the department"*.

In other words, they're expecting you to be bound by someone else's shitty negotiation skills, life problems (i.e. they got someone who desperately needed the job, has a shit-ton of alimony payments or child-support to make, or was otherwise defective).

This is NOT YOUR FUCKING PROBLEM. Keeping some limp-wristed, candy-ass simp—who took less than what he was worth— happy, is their problem. Your job is to MAXIMIZE your own income so you can pop Xanax, snort snow, and bang tight pussy on the weekend; like a normal fuck'n man.

Another slimy variation of this is if they give you some bullshit about how they *"Need it to evaluate your candidacy"*. Complete, fucking, bullshit it is! What they are trying to do is get you to give away all of your power and let them know how cheaply they can get you for. In addition, they probably think that your previous employer had your worth correct and value-pegged it right; they will cap you at that. Why they would think this way, when they all totally suck at calculating value, is beyond me. We all know by now, HR departments are hardly overflowing with this type of talent. You, by now, might be asking yourself, *"But Uncle McAvoy, what if the HR nitwits ask **three times** and won't continue my candidacy if I don't crack under pressure?"* A suitable question, indeed, from any young agent in the field.

My answer to you would be *"DO NOT force me go and look around for that sledgehammer, young Vassillie!"* Here is the deal, comrade. Any place that is *that* insistent is going to suck to work for. How can you tell? You can tell because even their HR drones suck more than usual. Oh, and here's another rule: Any place that demands a W-2 or 1099 verification is going to suck *so bad* that they might as well stick an "Arbeit Mach Frei" sign over their entryway.

I shit you not, they will probably be following you around after-hours to see if you are violating the company's "no sluts" rule.

Coming back to the other point, don't give them a salary range either. Let's say you're making $160k (I know, unrealistic, but the numbers are made up and the points don't matter anyways), comprised of a 90k salary and a 70k bonus. Now let's just assume that the company in question has budgeted for your position that you are applying at around $120-140k. If you tell them *"I earn a package worth $160k"* then you've priced yourself out of it for sure (which is probably a good thing, but maybe you're willing to take a 20k pay-cut to get away from your soul-destroying, coffee-breath bathing boss, or something). If you say *"I earn a salary of $90k, not including bonuses and benefits"* then you are some loser who isn't qualified enough for the position, otherwise you'd be making more.

Now, if they ask what your bonus is, well, that's a tricky one—since if they asked this, it means that you have already told them your base. Your answer should be "yes", but HR is not known for having creative thinkers. HR is known for having the "check the box" morons who just want to be done with you; so that they can go back to sleep in their 9-5 coffins until the sun goes down. Now, at some point, you may run into a hot chick in HR. They're usually very junior and will do things like show you to the conference room where your interview will take place, or fetch you coffee and or a Pellegrino.

They should, of course, be out locking down a man and having babies instead of wasting their good years in HR. What they are doing though is working some worthless job, doing nothing of real value to society, and complaining that they aren't paid enough. They've bought into the big lie of "GRRL POWER!" and will work that shitty job until around 28-29 when the first stirrings of rebellion escape from their uteruses and lay siege to their brains. Why these chicks don't figure out sooner that all of the women telling them how wonderful being an "Independent Career Wymyn!" is, are all miserable; single, post-wall, no-man-having Cat Colony Spinsters. It's beyond me. I digress...

How to Handle the "Salary" Question

As an initial matter, if you are applying anywhere that requires an application (some corporations are still stuck in the 1960's in this way), leave the "salary history" field blank, or put a ":P" in there. It's none of their fucking, business! When you get asked in an interview, answer in this manner: *"Once you have decided I am the right person for the job, I'm sure we will arrive at a number with which we are both happy"* Really, this should be the start and end of it.

However, it likely won't be. Nevertheless, you should stick to this position in that discussion of salary is premature at this stage of the game. If they want some comfort, tell them to tell you what they've budgeted for the position in question. This way you can decide whether or not you want to continue with the process. It's just a big game of poker between you and them and if you point out the fact that you know what they are trying to do, at least they know you're not retarded. This, they can respect you for.

Things to say, if you're a Bad-ass:

- *"I negotiate for a living [which you might] and if I answer this question, it means I'm a moron and you should disqualify me from further consideration."*
- *"I am not interviewing for my last/current job; I am interviewing for this job, which has more and different responsibilities."*
- *"I'm a lawyer...how much do you have?"*

- *"Do I look like a beautiful blonde with cantaloupe tittie and an ass that tastes like French Vanilla? No? Then why are you trying to fuck me!?"*

How to ask for a Raise

You are probably going to question down the line about how you are going to make more money at your current place of employment in CorporateLand.

The Short Answer:

You won't. The best way to move up the latter is to get off your current one, and move out.

The Long Answer: You can, however. Corporations,

like you've probably come to know, are not very good at determining employee value. It's because they're not really incentivized to. What they are incented to do is get you to work the most hours, for the cheapest price they can get for you. There are a couple of reasons for this. First, a lot of guys who run corporations are douchbags and it's not enough that they "win" by being overpaid assholes; it's that someone else has to "lose". That someone, dear comrade, is you. Second, it's too difficult to figure out how to value you in the business marketplace.

Remember, the Deportation Department (HR), is mostly populated by people of no value; so how are they suppose to know what value is, even if it's staring them in the face? Where are we going to stick all of the affirmative action hires? How about HR, where they really can't fuck anything up? Yeah, good choice, right? Seriously, I can't remember the last time I saw a male head of HR. Or a competent one.

The difficulty of valuing you is the one reason why HR always wants you to tell them, in the interview, how much money you are currently making or what your other employers valued you at. The assumption is that your last company pegged you just right and that is good enough for them to make "their own" assumption of your value. The economic environment is such that companies have to squeeze the fuck out of costs and the number one cost of a company is workers. This doesn't apply to the C-Suite of course, which is why the C-Suite still pays themselves a bag load of money while cutting the grunts down below. Some companies, particularly larger ones, will permit employees to transfer internally. Some of them make it easier, some make it harder (Backfill problems), and some require 2 years in your current job, whereas someone from the outside can simply walk in and apply. Thus, I'm not sure it's objectively better, even where internal candidates are "preferred"— right up until the candidates superior kills it because the person is too valuable in the situation, or just for the fun of it.

When to ask for the raise.

If your job responsibilities have changed in any way that makes you sweat more or take on more risk, whether substantially or enough to warrant it; particularly if you're already underpaid (which you probably are). If you didn't negotiate your initial salary correctly (their initial offer is always a premium for you and a discount for them) you are most likely working for them at a mark up. If you have closed a shit ton of sales/or deals, or if you have developed a new line of business, ask for a bigger slice of the corporate pie. In all serious though, you really need to find a "justifiable reason" for them to "make an exception" to whatever lockstep progression that they have going on.

Why is this case? Because if Cara McSmellypuss or Jack Mehoff get a whiff of your raise—and they will—they're going to want one as well because they were "hired at the same time" and they get all of their work done, and don't steal office supplies anymore: Never mind the fact that you come in at 7:00 am sharp and have landed four new "international accounts", while they roll in at a comfortable 9:20 am because the line at Starbucks is big.

How to ask. Look, if you stay in one place, they're going to try and give you the shitty 2-3% (merit increase). Most people will put up with the known "medium shitty" over the unknown of anything. The thing is battles are won before they are even fought. So, before you go have a sit-down and a "chat" with your boss, you need to do a few things first:

A) Figure out your worth in the marketplace. Use Glassdoor or whatever measure you wish, talk to head-hunters, and/or go on interviews—the last one gives you the best intelligence, but also know that you do run the risk of burning a few bridges.

B) Like in war, timing is everything. Don't ask for a raise in the middle of a layoff bonanza, or of course, right after you got a raise.

C) You should be tracking your accomplishments in your current outfit, and why you add more value than Wilma Flickerboob or Hugh Jass Wanker (without naming them by name of course). Be ready to make your case as if you were pitching a deal to the *Shark Tank*. Also, make sure you talk prospectively, not only about what you've already done. Point out if you will be taking on more new and more responsibilities in the future.

D) Never negotiate out of fear. This is why it is better to have a firm offer from somewhere else that you actually wouldn't mind going to before you commence negotiations. You don't have to reveal that you have an escape plan, but HAVE AN ESCAPE PLAN. Have a plan for all transitions and also more importantly down the road; have an EVAC plan from CorporateLand for good. The latter should have already been planned before you even started your tour of duty here. Remember, have a battle plan before you make the drop into enemy territory; your mission has to have an endgame. Just like how pilots use pre-sets and program their entire flight plan before the journey you need to do the same with your operations here in CorporateLand.

E) Handle money first. If you get a lot of resistance on more cash, or don't get as much as you want, start thinking about what you'd like to counter with in regards to non-cash "compensation". If your back is up against a hard cap on cash, ask for something else, like an extra week's vacation. Your boss and the company are operating from a position in which they don't want to give up more equity (control) than they have to in order to keep their workers productive and satisfied.

The thing is, you should be asking for more vacation time anyways, because, really, *time* is the most *valuable* commodity you have. You can always make more money, but once you spend your time, it's gone forever. Asking for more vacation time, is the same as asking for more "Shore leave" before you return to the War of the Cubicles. Every 9-5'er needs a little R&R—so that he doesn't go completely, fucking insane.

Some "Don'ts"

Let's imagine that I'm your boss for a moment. Let me tell you exactly what I'm thinking: *I DONT GIVE A FUCK why you "need" a raise. Organize your shit better. Get your fucking bitch wife to SPEND LESS. She's your problem, not mine.* Don't tell me WHAT you "deserve", tell me WHY. Don't give me an ultimatum; I might just fire you if I'm in a bad mood or you're already starting to piss me off as an employee these past few months. Don't get emotional, or raise your voice at me. Be cool and in control. Rehearse this conversation 100 times if you need to, in order to get there.

When to Bail If the company you're at isn't showing you the love you think you deserve, then pull the ripcord and move on. You may be thinking *"But wait sir, what if they make me a counter offer to stay?"* Fuck them, up the ass; without lube and with a red hot, iron poker. Besides, the "fishing for a counter-offer" strategy only works once, and thereafter you will always be a bit suspect, slippery. Beyond that, you then have to ask yourself *why they weren't showing you the love all along the way.* Why did you have to threaten to leave? They had plenty of time to take care of you and they only waited until they were going to lose you. Too little, too late, fuck them. This is war; this is *your* life we are talking about, not the fucking sandbox at daycare, or your report card from Grade 10.

Big Hill, Shiny Candy Mountain There is always the possibility that you *might* find a company that does not have its head completely up its own asshole, but that's not very likely today in CorporateLand; much has changed. Forward thinking and creative ingenuity is just not rewarded anymore or all that often, because of straight up autocracy and quarterly hand jobs. The other way is to work for a cool place that promotes you, or at least, finds a way to pay you more since you and your other co-workers are the veritable steam that drives the engine forward. Even if you put in tons of sweat equity, it's not going to translate into money, in a scalable way.

For example, let's just say that some years ago you did your job for 12 months and did someone else's job too (most likely a woman's because she was on Maternity leave). Do you think for even a second that you're going to get 1.5 x your current salary? No. Fucking. Way. You might get a bump in your bonus, which then can become the baseline for your bonus the following year, but in theory you left thousands in Sweat Equity on the table. However, it can pay off over time depending on your boss. This can happen if you work for a 'Big Hill, Shiny Candy Mountain' type of corporation where they do indeed value their workers and will recognize Sweat Equity. These types of companies operate under what is called the "Micheal's Model". They find talent, pay above market price for them, and then reap the rewards of having skilled, intelligent people, who have a lot of "institutional memory" because they've all been here for years fighting the good fight. They also promote from within.

Bottom Line

A) The best way to get a salary bump is to just change firms or companies.

B) You can get raises that are worth it where you are now, but it is generally hard as fuck and you're better off taking your value elsewhere.

C) Prepare, and have options. Don't negotiate out of fear and be ready to walk.

D) Your most valuable currency in your life is TIME. Do what you came to do in CorporateLand (make money) and make sure you get the fuck out as soon as your mission is over.

PROTOCOL| Four

Negotiations *for* Business

THIS SECTION OF TRAINING is mainly for commercial negotiations. It assumes some relative bargaining power—in examples that will be shown, typically I have superior knowledge, but the customer has the power to say yes— so in a way it's like a man trying to get a woman to spread for him. When I was in the corporate world, I negotiated for a living. Now, because of that, I try to train the best here in CorporateLand with my expertise. It's like the revolving door of the business world; once you're high up you don't really have to work anymore, just consult and teach what you know. That's why you're here—to learn from me, the best so that you can to survive. On any given day, upwards of 85% of what I do is psychology. The rest are facts and education about those facts. However, the psychology bit may be the most important thing anyone tells you about negations, heck, even about the corporate world in general.

While this may not be applicable for everyone—commercial negotiations— it is my hope that guys will find it's applications in their daily lives. We all negotiate in our daily lives whether or not we notice it at all, but it's there. We negotiate all the time; with our wives, our kids, the police officer, the dude at Best Buy or some chick you picked up at a bar somewhere.

It's all done either implicitly or explicitly. Lastly, I am basing this on negotiations in the West, America in particular. There will be differences across cultures. I sometimes handle things in other nations of the Anglosphere, but our cousins are not so different. In the past, I've done deals in Russia, where I have a slight advantage over other Westerners—I carry the Anglo-Irish last name of my father's family, so I can be a bit of a surprise to Slavs. However, they eventually come around to a moment of sincerity that typically takes the form of, *"Troy. You are not like other Westerners. You are deep like us."* I am always amused, but in a sincere sort of way.

The Basics of Negotiations

Before any negotiation, you have to understand who you're dealing with first, if they have the power to say "yes" or if they are just the gatekeeper, and whether or not they come from a negotiation culture and what that culture is. What is your risk tolerance? What is your counterparts risk tolerance?

What are your "must haves"? What are theirs? When are you figuring this all out? That leads me to my first point.

Preparation

"Failure to prepare, is preparing to fail."— Winston Churchill. If possible, try to spend (at minimum) 30 minutes before a negotiation session, preparing; Going over the opening points, going over any previous concessions by the other party, etc. Know your paper and theirs inside and out and that you can quote it from memory. In one gig, I was so familiar with a primary counterparty's paper that I could tell you where all the typos were. So I don't feel at a disadvantage if I don't have as much time to prepare as I'd like.

Control the Paper

This isn't always possible to do but when it is, use it. When I was working in the hell hole grind, I'd let our clients redline the fuck out of it. I love it when they do that. It lets me see into their minds, what they want, what they are afraid of, etc. No worries, though—I use my powers only for good, and not for evil.

When negotiating, it is imperative to understand what the other person is *afraid* of and that will also reveal in time what they ultimately want. Just like in dating with women, if you know a woman's particular agenda then you can decide if you want to pursue business with her and whether or not she is worth your time and energy. 90% of the time, I was dealing with someone I had superior knowledge over— my industry was specialized and I had been in it a long, fucking time. I would usually try to establish myself as the "kindly Uncle," who wasn't out to screw them. And you know what? Usually I was not out to screw them. Why? In an industry that was extremely price sensitive we had to restrain a ridiculously high percentage of our customers, and you restrain customers by keeping them happy. I've had guys go chasing a nickel or a dime, but odds are 6-12 months later, I would see those guys again because the guy who they gave their business to fucked them. My goal was to be "Steady Eddie"—make my margin, return client phone calls, and no surprises on their bills.

Never Negotiate out of Fear

This can't bear enough repeating. The best time to buy a new job or car is when you have a job, or car that runs. Sales guys get itchy when we're down to the end, because their loyalty is to the deal. I've had them get all spun up about a customer asking for something stupid and me saying no. *"But, what if they walk over this?!"*

I wish I had a dollar for every time I've heard that. If I was in a cruel mood I would reply, *"Then you don't get fucking paid. But I do."* What I usually go with is, *"When was the last time we had a client walk over [whatever]? Would that be a 'Never'?"* Incidentally, I have never once had a deal collapse at the end because I didn't give in on a customer's nutty last minute request.

Know What Your Risk Tolerance Is. If you

don't want any risk, don't do any business. That is what CorporateLand is all about, risk. That's what it was set-up for—men who take risks to reap the extravagant rewards that came with it. That said you don't have to be crazy either. Proper risk controls have saved more firms than they've cost, although you will lose deals from time to time.

What Does The Other Party Want?

This is particularly useful when it's something I don't care about, because I will attach a concession it. If it's that fucking important to him, then there should be some juice in it for me. With that said, be as fair as you can, within your parameters. It will keep your customers coming back. I remembered guys who did me a solid. And, I also never forgot guys who fucked me over, more so.

Negotiation Culture

Middle Easterners, Russians, guys who are afraid they're getting ripped off, lawyers who think that any idea proposed by the other side's lawyer is automatically bad. There are also gender differences among lawyers. Women are the worst. They are also often the best. There are three women right now that I deal with directly and regularly who are a pure joy to work with. They are that way because *I* picked them. They know what to ask for, what not to ask for and their "emotional intelligence" in dealing with their clients—and me— are quite high. On the other hand, I've also had women attorneys— and I have never ONCE had a male attorney do this— come back to the table after 95% of everything was finished and say, " *I was thinking about this last night, and I want to reopen discussions on [Fucking EVERYTHING]...*" That gets a "*HELL,* no."

Don't be afraid to say "No" If you don't like the

deal, and you can't get it on terms that work for you, and then just simply walk away. It's seldom the end of the world. This is, incidentally, how I treat car buying or women. The dealership will be there tomorrow and another woman will walk around the corner.

The dealership will have more and better cars to sell tomorrow than the previous day and more girls are turning a ripe 18 everyday around the world, in no short order. So, if I don't like the deal, I walk. I also establish my street cred, first (i.e. I'm the sole decision maker). I don't have a wife telling me I can't have a Porsche or whatever, and if I get the deal I want, I'm dropping the hammer on it. I also don't fall in love with deals, not cars, women or anything else. If it's not working for me, I sell or don't do the deal at all. Don't like the deal? Adjourn and reconvene later.

Never Let the Dumbest Guy Dictate the Terms

Never let the dumbest guy in the room tell you the score or what is best for you. This really sucks when it's the other side's decision maker, but sometimes that's how it is. In such cases I wind up dealing with our sales guys and have to drive two points home: *"I'm sorry Steve doesn't get it, but the next time I give on [term] will be the FIRST time."* I will often remind our sales guys that, *"Well I guess you'll have to, you know, SELL."* That can be a bit of a dick move, but our guys also know that when I refuse a term, there's a reason, and I'm not just saying 'no' because I'm afraid or because I don't understand something.

Don't Revel Many years ago, when I was just a young lawyer (yeah, I was a lawyer too), I was trying to work out a deal for a client who had fucked things up so badly, royally actually. My position was bad, and there wasn't a "blow up" option that wasn't worse.

It truly, sucked. Even worse, the lawyer I was dealing with was a guy who was really full of himself. Not only was he a raging dickhead on some of the terms where it was just unnecessary, but he made a point of rubbing my face in it at the conclusion. What could I do? I had a weak position and blowing things up wasn't an option. The thing is your "Kindly Uncle" Troy has a long memory. How long? When the elephants forget what type of a shit they took yesteryear, they come to me. So, months went by and, wouldn't you know it? I had another matter with the same guy. And guess who had the whip hand this time around? I was an absolute *bastard* on every little detail. And then sometimes, on points that were settled, I would suddenly "change my mind" and ask for more concessions! I would always be very emotionless and surgical about it, and never blew my cool. Why? Because never blow your cool. Let the other guy blow his cool, and look like a dick. So, did I fuck him? Motherfucking right I did! Long and hard, without lube. My cock was, metaphorically, so far up his shit pipe that it was bumping into the inside of his skull. Everyone knew about it, too. How? Dumb fucker couldn't stop complaining about me to anyone who would listen to him.

Now, discussing client matters isn't smart to begin with, but why advertize a loss to your colleagues? Since I have huge connections in Russia, let's just say I had a few dudes 'pay him a visit' and *actually* fuck him up, physically. Nobody messes with guys like me if you know who I am and what I'm capable of. This guy clearly *didn't* and he paid the price, with his life. He's most likely not practicing law anymore; as his body should be at the bottom of the Hudson right now, or on a barge somewhere to the orient.

If you want to see sympathy, it's in the dictionary between "shit" and "syphilis". I also had a reputation as a deal maker, so I had guys I knew calling up and asking why I had done what I did, which gave me a chance to put the word out myself. That was important because...

A Good Reputation is a Mighty Shield

Within my profession community and separately, my social life, I can go places other people could only dream of. Do things other people can't and talk to certain people other's couldn't— even on their best of days in this world; all without arousing suspicion. Why/how? It's because in those *milieus*, I am a "known Guy". If I give you my word on something, it's 24k. I'm particularly careful about it though; because if you *blow it just once*, things will never be the same. This is what you should aspire to become if you want to make it here.

Brutal Honesty

I had a call once go waaaay to fucking long. A more experienced me would have cut it off much sooner; but back in the early days we didn't really have mentors like *you* do now, with me. It involved a Middle Eastern and an Asian counterparty making stupid, fucking, demands. Finally, I said, *"Look, I live like ten minutes from the office. I have nowhere else to go and nothing else to do today. You are NOT going to wear me down. Ten minutes after this phone call, I will be sitting down to a hot meal. We can either start making progress, or I can hang up and go have dinner, your call."* This is another one where you have to be careful in how you play it. I had a nervous client, but one who was mollified by me telling him, *"You can have a shitty deal right now, or you can have a good deal in 24-48 hours. Tell me which one you want."*

Department *of* Deportation

THE HARDEST PART about surviving in CorporateLand is being aware of the landmines and potential booby-traps that are hidden and laying around the field in the form of policies, regulations, and double-agents known as Social Justice Warriors. Let's start with some obvious landmines.

Alcohol The number one way to fuck up your otherwise awesome career is substance abuse. It was never like this before. Back in the Golden Years, you could drink at the office and even have your own liquor cart to which you would use every time a dude came in to chat about Peggy's tits—and how they would look great with your face buried between them.

It used to be that we'd all go out, get shit-faced, and misbehave. There was an unspoken agreement that, the next day, everyone would pretend it didn't happen; even if late nights call for bail money had to be made. Sadly, those days are over, thanks to the pussification of CorporateLand.

Now you will get fired for even thinking about staring at Fiona's figure, having any indiscretion in the workplace, or even outside on social media and in physical reality. Even the *appearance* of such "misbehavior" is enough to cut your throat. How then, *do you*, not get too drunk and behave like a rampaging dickhead? Happily, there are a number of ways you can maneuver around this.

First, I read somewhere, about someone famous, always having a drink in his hand at parties: The same one he was handed by the host when he arrived. He would simply nurse that for hours. Fine, if that's what you want to do.

Second, if you set a limit based on your tolerance and comfort level this is also fine. That limit should be 0-2 drinks, inclusive. After that, ask for a glass of soda/tonic with a lemon or lime wedge. Nobody will know the difference and after a couple of pops, nobody will either.

Third, if all else fails, never be drunker than the 3rd drunkest person at the party. This is not the Olympics and you do not want to be on the medal stand for the ceremony. The gold medalist will draw the most shit on the next business day and will get the most coverage. The silver and bronze guy will catch some heat as well for their achievement. If you're 4th or lower, you should mostly be ok.

Holiday Parties

These are joyless affairs now that fit nicely into the Hobbes' description of life: Nasty, Brutish and Short. Going to an office holiday party today, versus a normal party, is like visiting the Eastern Bloc during the 80's and early 90's; it's not as bad as it was during the 1940's, but it's still depressing as fuck. They are often interminable.

The plot basically comes down to: *People who don't like each other, standing around uncomfortably, eating food they don't want to eat, drinking things they don't want to drink and talking about things they would rather not talk about.* So, what do you do in that situation? I treat holiday parties like I would treat any other "family function": Get in, tell a few jokes, relive the old times, and then get out before it blows and someone gets hurt.

Typically, these things are structured as dinners. That's fine. Eat, drink (a little) be merry (but not too merry) and then pull the ripcord/pop purple smoke and call for an EVAC. If the event starts by 19:00 hrs or 20:00 hrs, your mission should be to get out by 21:00 or 22:00. Your momma was right, boy! Nothing good ever happens after 10 pm. If you have a date and someone doesn't want you to leave, then it's because *she's not feeling well*. Men, older men like bosses, will never question that because what if it's 'Female troubles'? Exactly, we treat that shit like Kryptonite. Or you can just leave.

I used to work with a guy, let's call him Chet MegaSplooge; because that's what his name should've been. Chet was a great guy. He was a great guy even when he was hit'n the sauce. He was a great guy until he came across "A Drink Too Far". Then he just plain became evil Chet. Seriously, this guy would turn on a dime. He'd go from being your best bud and comrade to getting the evil "Private Pyle" look from *Full Metal Jacket* and taking a swing at you. So at a Christmas party, I saw him by the bar, naturally. I stopped to say hello, just as the "Drink Too Far" arrived from the barkeep. From that point I sort of knew shit was going to get bad, that the air raid sirens would start to go off, and that it was time to head to the bunkers and wait out Chet's inevitable rampage on the field. Guy's like Chet are always the problem—the fresh out of college, dude-bro-dude's, who think it's a 'Won in Best' contest— of who has the most daddy issues.

Anyway, he looked like he was going to take a swing at me for no reason, and I was going to have to step out of the way so that his follow-through would carry him past me—one of our co-workers arrived on scene, and I took that opportunity to beat feet and head to safety. So, anyway, two dudes tried to EVAC him into a cab that was called in. He was hammered and suffering from the booze as it was leaking from his mouth; staining his White shirt. He even tried to take a swing at the other two 9-5'ers trying to get him into the transport. Kicking and screaming ensued; cries of even came from Chet's mouth asking for someone to get his drink for him (he didn't want to leave it behind). It was a sad scene, a solemn day.

So, the next day at work he had a shot at saving his job, but he came in still hammered and started arguing with his superior, who stopped the meeting after five minutes and fired him on the spot; discharged from the firm. Don't Be That Guy. Don't be Chet.

Gifts and Gratuities

The ultimate Sphincter Police— you know the type... *"But...but...but that might look bad!!"* the kind of turds and maggots you want to punch in the face for being so pussified—have absolutely ruined corporate gift giving. So basically, when it comes down to gifts and more commonly, business dinners, everyone ass-rapes their corporate policy and shuts the fuck up about it. There are more often times than not a "per person" cap on business dinners, so what happens is the guy running the dinner just adds people.

Business Dinners

We will cover later how to effectively be the Master of business dinners, but here is the general lowdown. Another thing the pencil-pushers have tried to ruin is corporate dinners. The third and fourth time one of the firms here got bought, the new openers put in a per-person limit on dining expenses. The solution: Suddenly, there is twice the number of people at dinner now when going out. I asked a VP once if he enjoyed dinner one night at *Maison*. He demurred that he had not been there at all, to which I replied, *"Oh, well...you're going on the expense report."* That was in front of the CEO, who chuckled. Your enemy in all of this is the Evil Expense Goblins. They are little pinheaded morons who think they have totally scored by disallowing an expense. They seriously beat off at night with a full bottle of baby oil at the thought of catching someone charging an in-room movie. It's that bad. The best case scenario: To up the quality of your meals, is to have a VIP customer or client with you. We have a guy who sends us eight figures a year, and that first number isn't a "1". He get's whatever, the fuck, he wants. If he wanted to go to an Italian restaurant *in Italy* and have two chicks blow him while he's cutting a meat ball in half, I'm *pretty* convinced we could find a way to make it happen.

The more unassailable your companions are, the easier your reporting life will become to the Expense Goblins. I used to have a friend at Amex (American Express) who would put me ahead of the line on short notice at hard-to-get restaurants.

The caveat was I'd have to use my personal Amex because he knew my account backwards and forwards and if he ever got crap for it, he needed to be able to pull up the numbers, show his superior that we'd dropped a shit ton of green on wine, etc. The Expense Goblins don't like this. Why? It's because we had gotten corporate cards along the way and it was thereafter 'Verboten' (sieg heil!) to use personal cards for corporate expense. So, *vat* to do? This is one case where I asked permission first, rather than begged for forgiveness, later. I was the go-to guy at the company for the upper right-hand part of CorporateLand. If it happens north of DC and east of Indiana, it's got my greasy little prints all over it. So, I shot a note off to my admin and everything was cool as Siberian shit. The dinner went great, client was happy, and my expense report...got rejected. Fuck tits. That was Five and ½ Large on my personal, fucking, credit card. Fuck. Now, the Expense Goblins are not known for being creative thinkers. That's why they do what they do. So, my poor admin had been trying to get this approved and kept getting nowhere, mostly because she was a sweetheart. So, I had her forward the email chain to me, and sure enough, all the way at the bottom was the approval. So, I shot a note back to the head Goblin with the following note:

"Please. Scroll down to the bottom where you will find the following message: 'Approved. Daddy BigBalls'. That's who my next phone call is going to. Let me know how you wish to proceed."

Translation: *"Hey, fuckhead. I realize that mother nature and genetics have given you a brain the size of a raisin, that has never been used, but you have ten minutes to get your head out of your ass and your hand off your small prick or you're getting fired. I'm counting backwards starting.....now."*

Five minutes later, I got a message back "This is approved". No shit it was approved, Shirlock.

Sex, Religion, Politics

Sex

It's a workplace, not a singles bar or night club. Sure, it'd be fun to nail Patricia in Payroll, who plays beach volleyball during the summer and tennis on Sunday's— who has a savage tan and superbly toned ass. Perhaps it's worth it to nail her, *I* don't know. On the other hand, all it takes is her feeling "weird" about *you* one day and you're fucking toast, my friend. If you do want to fish for prime tuna off the company pier, it would be better for you to pick someone who has more to lose than you do. Also, be wary of engaged women or women at the office who are going through a "rough patch" with their "asshole" of a boyfriend.

Note: Engaged women are fun to watch and study. They seem to go through a phase, by which, Acquisition of Engagement Ring and Wedding Ring where they need constant validation of their continued appeal to men who are not their future husbands. Maybe not every one of them, but it's definitely a trend. They still want to be seen as fuckable, even though they are settling, quitting life and presumably the sexual market place (for the time being as marriages have a 50% survival rate if lucky). So, you might score, or she may pull the old *"What?! You KNOW I am engaged to be married to [insert 'Dad-bod' nerdy guy]"* I don't recommend it unless you are looking to hand in your 2 week's notice for good in CorporateLand.

Oh, and here's how crazy women can be. I know a woman who works down on Wall Street, at a well-known bank. If you name out loud the first four of the big five financial institutions you can think of it, it will be one of those. Anyway, she's an admin and started fucking some guy she works with on the regular; getting dat pussy tapped like a tree up in Canada for maple syrup. And she's totally cool about the whole thing at the beginning. Fast forward a month or so later, the dude's wife finds out about his lumber-jacking trials with this admin chick and raises all Holy Hell. She [the wife of this guy] basically *forces* this dude—who, as it turns out, is a massive pussy—to make it a "work issue".

She [the wife] also rats out my admin friend to her husband; they were amicably separated and in the process of divorcing and he couldn't have given a shit. That's how vengeful this cunt was. So what happened?

The guy was actually on track for big things at his company. HR calls in my admin friend and asks *"What do you want?"* And pretty much what she wanted was going to happen. Think about that for a bit; let it simmer into that Green, rookie brain of yours. She basically said that she wanted all of the bullshit to go away, to keep working there at the company and she wasn't going to complain; would basically be a good citizen of CorporateLand. They transferred the guy from HQ to an office that was *maybe* 45 min away, but it might as well have been Siberia. Or the fucking moon. He was going to make the money he was already making, but his fast track career ended the day he started pounding my friends poon into oblivion and more importantly; the day he let his crazy ass wife start making all of his work decisions for him!

So guy's, if you're going to fuck around and get caught (which you probably will) don't let your wife decide your work fait (other than divorce). Actually, *don't* even get married in the first place; which will eliminate that liability at the very least. If you're married, you can bet your ass you will be stuck in CorporateLand for the rest of your life and you will die here without question, I've seen it many times.

In closing for this section, there is a >99% chance that you can bonk a chick from work and nothing bad happens. However, it's like kidnapping; it's a low frequency/**high impact** event. When you're caught, the entire Deportation Department responds en masse with every available unit and it's either suicide or death by shootout. Mike MegaStar at the office might survive it, but you, noob, are not yet Mike MegaStar.

Religion

If you've found Jesus or God then that's great for you; ask him WTF is up with kids getting cancer and why he seems to send all of the hurricanes and tornadoes to destroy trailer parks, and finally: Women. Massive design flaw on his part or did he do that shit on purpose to annoy us? Then ask him if he can turn the water cooler into a keg so I can at least be drunk as fuck when all the Jesus tards start worshiping themselves at work. The only acceptable mentions of religion are *"Oh, our wedding is at 'Our Lady of Perpetual Responsibility & Liability' parish in June,"* or *"The baptism will be held at St. Matthews Church for Wayward Girls"* .Otherwise, nobody gives a flying fuck, and those that do will be "offended" by it, most likely.

Politics

This also is a do-not-touch topic these days. It used to be that if you disagreed with your neighbor about politics that was O.K. You'd make fun of each other and go back to being friends. Now everyone seems to get their Man Panties in a twist up over with it; and don't get me started on the women.

I was out with a hard-core evangelical that I worked with, who quite sensibly understands to keep his opinions to himself, for the most part. The two guys on the other side of the table were from a consultant firm, and one of them chose to lead off with his deep abiding hatred for George W. Bush. He even knew he shouldn't have, because he said so; all the while his partner was giving him the death stare of *Will you for fuck sakes, STOP FUCKING TALKING.* So I waited for a pause and said "Yes, but on the other hand, I understand that he has a fine singing voice." So the guy looked at me like, 'What?' and I said, "Oh, I have no idea if he does or not, but you were clearly trapped in a death spiral and I was trying to give you a parachute to pull on" that broke the tension and the conversation moved on to business, like it should.

You'll never know what the beliefs of your customer/client/counterparty/business partner are and these days you don't want to find out the wrong way.

Travel like Jason Borne & Learning the Art *of* Business Trips

I LIVE ON THE WEST COAST mainly, like others I know here in CorporateLand. We frequently travel from one coast to the other (and sometimes Europe) at the behest of our employers. You will also do the same someday as you rank up here during your stay. I've logged over a million miles in the air, which, while it doesn't qualify me as a *true* road warrior anymore like the old days, I've learned a lot about making my life easier while up in the air and in strange beds. There is definitely a certain art, if you will, to traveling during your stay in the corporate world; some do it well and others like me did it the best. Business trips can be one of the most brutal things you'd have to go through; however, it doesn't have to be that way, not with a little imagination and fortitude.

Getting Dispatched I have a rule these days: Either I'm in Business Class, or I'm **not** fucking going. Why? Because like any normal human being, I like comfort. I like pre-boarding and I *especially* like free booze. I also have zero interest in sitting in steerage. Coach class seats must have been designed by Alfred P. Southwick. Fuck it.

You don't want me in one of those either if you have the misfortune of sitting adjacent to you. From the time I was thirteen years-old, my shoulders have been broader than a fucking coach seat, so I either lean out into the aisle or my shoulder is going into the ear of the sad-faced, unlucky person sitting next to me. So, how do you set out about it? If you are going to be doing side missions regularly with you company, you might have a corporate travel department that makes arrangements for you. If so, you have my utmost sincere condolences, because they don't give a *shit* about your care and comfort. If you're fortunate enough, they'll care about getting you to where you're going, when you get there, how many connections you have or where you sit—and trust me, the only reason to sit in the last row of the aircraft is because you have a massive case of diarrhea or you want to become friends with people who do. During my stay here in CorporateLand I have only worked at one place that insisted that I use their provider. I would choose my bookings and tell them to book them. They wouldn't listen of course, but happily they were sloppy, so once I had demonstrated that I could find better routings at lower cost, I was exempted.

More freedom, more comfort, no bullshit. You'll find in life and in CorporateLand that when you are as smart as someone like me, other people tend to become a real issue in regards to your happiness. Companies will often have rules and regulations about when you can fly Elite or Business Class, otherwise, it's Cattle Class. Where I was stationed mainly it used to be Coach only, until one of the big poohbas had to fly a lot of trans-continentals. Suddenly, if you were in the air for four fucking hours you could fly Business.

I used to defeat this by booking Y-Class (the most expensive coach fare) and then buying an upgrade (often for very little money) or use miles, and volia!, I'm in Business, figuratively and literally. I'd make sure it was papered up; meaning I could produce a receipt for Coach Class, and then the Expense Goblins could go back to sleep in their 9-5 coffins.

Air travel isn't majestic like in the old days; unless you fly on Singapore, Cathay, Emirates, Eithad or, lately, Turkish Airlines (so I hear). There are reasons for grouping your travel under the aegis of Alliance. There are three major alliances: Star Alliance [United, Lufthansa, Austrian, Scandinavian, Swiss, Singapore, Turkish plus some others. Skyteam you have [Delta, Air France, KLM, Aeroflot, Aeromexico, Alitalia, KAL, Czech and some others]. With OneWorld you have [American, BA, Cathay, JAL, Qantus, Qutar, and others].

There are some notable independents, though: Emirates, Etihad, Virgin Atlantic, Iceland Air as well as LCCs (low cost carriers) such as Ryan Air, Jet Blue, South West, etc. Virgin Atlantic is 49% owned by Delta and so miles can be directed to one's Delta account, and if memory serves correct, Jet Blue has some deal with Etihad, but unless you're flying a lot to the Middle East through to India, it's not going to matter very much at all. Which one you pick is based entirely on what your destinations, both domestic and foreign, will be. If it's Atlanta, Paris and New York, welcome to the Skyteam. If it's going to be Berlin, Chicago and Singapore you're flying with; hello, Star Alliance. London & New York? Congrats, you can pick from just about anyone.

There are a few knots and wrinkles though. For example, I met a Brit once on a KLM flight and found it was odd that he was on KLM, as he lived in England. As it turns out, KLM has a city hopper flight from AMS to somewhere midlands sounding that drops him into an airport 15 minutes from his house. So, all of his trips to the States are on Skyteam affiliates. Go figure. I am something of a Skyteam detainee, because my transcons for work are best made on Delta airlines in terms of convenience and usually price. Most of my foreign travel is to Europe, so I try to route through either AMS or— and this surprises a lot of people—Moscow! Skyteams other Western European hub, CDG in Paris, is a bit of a clusterfuck.

It's poorly designed and it's run by the French. That airport is also considered to be a black hole for checked baggage. It's much better to use Amsterdam; home of the friendly, efficient, America-loving (or at least best at faking it), and perfectly willing-to-speak-English Dutch. London is more of a destination for me, so I either fly Delta or Virgin airlines—Virgin's "Clubhouses" are always top-banana.

So, why do I use the Russkies as a connecting airport? Delta formerly flew there, non-stop. Now it's Aeroflot. Aeroflot's pricing is typically favorable, and I can also flirt with the stewardesses in Russian. The food and accommodation is comparable to a big Western airline, and it's a 9-10 hour flight mind you; which means I can have dinner, watch a movie and get 6 hours of shut-eye— which is all I need most days. Even better, when I hop back over to Europe from SVO, it's on a plane with a proper Business Class, rather than just Coach or some other configuration with the middle class seat blocked out. Now that SVO has been built out due to increased air traffic and demand, it's now a modern fucking airport. There won't be as many English-speakers, but if you're jammed up, usually someone will help you along. On one of my last transfers, the chatter didn't speak a lick of English, but I overheard a young American in line in front of me asking them for the location of the nearest bar and toilets, so I leaned forward and answered her question in English.

Also, the Russkies aren't politically correct (thank fucking, God), so I usually breeze through security without even opening my laptop bag; but I suspect if I looked like Bindar's cousin, things might have gone differently. The Russians aren't pussies and they don't fuck around. That's why nobody fucks with them.

Frequent Flyer or Frequent Fleer?

So once you've sussed out what airlines you will be flying with, it's time to sign up for those airlines' frequent flyer programs. The only active ones I have at the moment are Delta and United. There is a distinction to be drawn between "miles" and "qualification miles", the latter are what's important. They are sometimes called "BiS" miles by road warriors, which is short for "Butt-in-seat". Typically, those are the ones that count in determining 'statuses with an airline and with status come perks. There are a few other ways to get "qualification miles", but those are typically the result of spending exorbitant amounts on personal credit cards, or "topping-up" at the end of the year.

By-pass the Herd, Be a Knife through Butter

In case you've been living in ditch somewhere, airports are now complete, fucking, zoos. The trick is to get enough frequent flyer swag to get to use the better-trained humans at the Elite-priority-whatever counters.

Generally, you have to be at least a "Gold" or 2nd tier up from all the plebs. You should really be ticketing yourself at home, preferably by printing your boarding pass to PDF, so you can e-mail it to your admin for your expense report. I also like to carry a paper ticket in case something goes wrong, because knowing this world, it does and probably will—dead battery, no bars, whatever.

When you check your baggage—and try to avoid this as much as possible since it's a pain in the fucking ass now—leave them with the nice person at the Elite counter, then head on over to security. This is always much more of a hassle than it needs to be, but they're really trying to put on a Floor Show for Ma and Pa Mckettle from the Midwest. The bottom line is, if some sand rat, motherfucking camel jockey, gets up and yells *"Allah kbar!"* it's basically up to the dudes on the plane to make him eat their fists, and stomp on his face until said sand rat's skull performs a fascinating transition into the concave variety. When you're up in the air, you're on what police call "YOYO" time—you're on your own. Essentially, a better way to handle security is to get TSA-pre. The government already has a shit ton of information on you, and always...has; now they're just better at organizing it. So why not just put it to work for you? Basically, you will fill out a form, they figure out if you're a BAD GUY somehow—criminal record, fondled some kids behind a Dairy Queen, hang out with Sand People in Syria; or some other obvious honey-moon capital of the world where pieces of complete-fucking shit congregate—then they either give it to you or not.

I travel overseas and so it comes with my Global Entry, which lets me cut the line at immigration and customs and use the kiosks. So, because I don't check bags, it takes me a cool 15 minutes from the plane to landside, rather than being tossed about like a dinghy on a sea of Third-World'ers meandering about like the shit-wicks they are. Plus, not have to deal with all the domestic dummies in the "Citizens" lane. The worst part is when there are cordoned lanes before you get into the arrival section because there is always some dumbass that has to stop and think shit over, clogging things up.

TSA—Pre probably comes with SENTRI also, which is for people who go to Mexico for whatever reason, and NEXUS is the same thing, only for Canada. My understanding is that if you are a GE and you bring your GE card you can use SENTRI lanes on land crossing with Mexico. However, I really only care about immigration at airports and getting through security more quickly. The great news is, while the TSA aren't anything near great, it's better than the fucking losers they had working airport security before; who were working there because they couldn't hold down a job at McDonald's or a 7-11. Ideally, the Pre-check line will be way shorter and quicker, because you don't have to take your shoes off, have your toothpaste in a stupid plastic bag or whatever. Active duty military personnel who are in uniform can use the Pre lanes, which I'm totally fine with.

If there is a nutter or Suicide Camel-fucker on my flight, I want them to think twice or just have the military dude and Air Marshall curb-stomp them; turning their face into a bowl of human fondue. Once you are inside the Wall, your next move is to have enough street-cred to get into an airport club. While they don't have creamy tanned strippers and Beef Wellington on the grill, like back in the old days, there tends to be fewer screaming children, some kind of decent booze (free) and some snacks at least. Delta now lets you pay for their "Premium" booze—the stuff they charge for—with miles, which is nice.

You can get in by flying business or first on an international flight, or by having the right plastic; whether it's a club pass that you buy, or is gifted to you by the airline. Also, if you have a high enough status with one of their partner liners or the right type of credit card, usually Amex Platnium or Centurion—which got you into everything but Admirals Clubs, but now only works, IIRC, at Delta's SkyClubs. Diners Club—which is still in existence, evidently—has a decent network of second-tier clubs. Then there is Priority Pass which is like Diners only not as decent. Amex is building out its own network of clubs and the few that I've been to, are pretty sweet.

Clubs also, in most cases, have the benefit of having agents who can tend to your travel needs for changes or re-bookings etc., while the Great Unwashed are waiting in a long-ass line at the counter. It won't be Holly and her sweet pneumatic titties anymore, but alas, the Golden Years have come and gone; because wanting half-naked dancers in a Club lounge is apparently sexist, yet, strutting around in skin-tight yoga pants, camel-toe, is any different? This world is insane.

On the positive side of things, some airports that I've been in that are a bit better than a bus station in Rio *but* have great club rooms for some reason. Vienna used to be like that. It was either persuade your way into the club—and experience civilization— or suffer and watch the Olympic lice race happening on the gentleman's (of indeterminate origin) head, sitting far too close to you on the outside. I went into the club there and drank some Martel cognac—in Charles Martel's honor—while I laughed at all the peons on the outside.

Side Tip: Later in that year I had to be in Istanbul from time to time. With relatively little hassle, I was able to get Turkish Airlines to do a status match—they will match mid-tier and top-tier status from a competing alliance team in their program. I don't care so much about upgrades, but that mid-tier on Turkish gets me in to Star Alliance clubs that I would otherwise be able to utilize. To keep it for the next two years, all I have to do is fly just one international trip on Turkish in the next couple of months, or whatever. I'll bust that nut off by March.

Before the Green Light

Down at the gate, try to arrive 5-10 minutes early. Whatever the boarding time, it's going to be probably 5-10 minutes before they embark. If you're in business or have the right status, they will let you on the plane first— but *try* to stand to the side and play nice— after they board all the handicappers, gimps and old-farts (who can barely remember where they are). Then there are gate lice hanging about—because everyone thinks there's an "exception" and everyone thinks that exception applies to them. On board, stow your gear and relax. The peons will be boarding after you, while you enjoy your Old Fashion and settle in.

The Art *of* Flipping a Hotel into a Vacation Villa

YOU'RE NOT ALWAYS GOING to be stationed within CorporateLand for your entire tour-of-duty. Sometimes you will be dispatched to other foreign lands for the greater good of the mission of your company. These secondary operations will provide you the opportunity for some R&R while you're still slaying and executing your corporate mandate. Your primary goal should be to make your stay here as seamless as possible; just like in your normal life. Traveling for the corporation doesn't have to be depressing or lack a certain flare, you just have to be creative. Conveniently, with high-end hotels, that's their goal as well.

The higher-end the hotel, or the more socialist the economy in whatever country you find yourself in, the more likely you're going to meet people on staff who are in the service as a career and not because its summer and their university is on break. If you get to know the "lifers", that is going to break in your favor. Stay in the same place in each city, or same chain of hotels.

That is the first ingredient you will need to live like a Maharajah on the road. If you find yourself visiting the same city when being dispatched from your CorporateLand HQ, try and stay at the same hotel each time; such that they get to know you and you get to know them. Also, just as airliners have frequent flyer programs; hotels have frequent guest programs as well. In the United States, the largest and most well-known are Starwood Preferred Guest, Marriot Rewards, Hilton HHonors, IHG Rewards Club and Hyatt Gold Passport. The trick is to lump your hotel stays such that you become a top-tier member of a particular chain's program, which will then entitle you to perks when you then use that chains hotels for *personal* travel as well—which is, for me anyway, the point. You doing this, while you're serving CorporateLand, will effectively pay dividends down the road when you've retired and ended your tour of duty.

The points standing and rewards you've racked up traveling on company time and dime will then be there for you after the war in the cubicle trenches. All of your road warrior stays at Marriott Courtyards can pay off when you're travelling on your own later on in life and would like to stay at the Ritz. I use Hyatt and SPG, and sometimes Marriot as well as Taj, which is big in India; but last I knew of only had 3 hotels in the U.S. Use Hyatt because it only takes 50 nights to get into the top-tier. I then use the points I accumulate on business travel for when I travel on my leisure time to places that have Park Hyatts, etc.

They have nice hotels where *I* want to travel to, and Hyatt's program also allows a Diamond member to book a suite upgrade 4x for up to 7 nights each time. Hyatt also lets you use the "Cash & Points" option in conjunction with the suite upgrades—typically with most hotels that's an 'either-or'—so , instead of booking a solid $300 room and upgrading to a suite, you're booking a $125 room and upgrading to a suite, which is nice for when it's time for some R&R, fun in the sun. Other people prefer Marriott's or Starwood. Doesn't matter. Marriot is nice because they own Ritz Carlton...they are also about to own Starwood. Once you know which hotel group you're going to go with and be utilizing the most, it's time to learn the program and act accordingly. One of the reasons I so often get what I want from airlines and hotels is because I make it easy for them to say *yes* to me, and so should *you*, young comrade. How?

By not being a huge, total raging dickhead and by understanding their program and what they can do for you and me. Thus, I frequently suggest options to them, in such cases where the *need* arises.

How to Choose a Villa So, how do you decide whether you will like a particular villa or not? Well, do you like the bar?—Always a great indicator and my personal favorite when it comes to gut instincts. One of my absolute favorite hotels has three, yes *three*, bars and a lounge with a restaurant (with a great fucking breakfast!). Also, they have a pool that is top-banana; thus it is my "Villa" of choice. Every time I arrive, the guest relations manager greets me and checks me in herself—unless she's not working that shift and then her deputy does. Same goes for the restaurant. There is something to be said with having a routine or preference for certain things when it comes to ordering food and drink. Usually, it's recommended that you remain unpredictable, as a man, in your social and also in your profession somewhat to have an edge. However, if your favorite waitress', at the restaurants you normally go to, knows your order or even knows your choice of drink off by heart—and brings that drink to you almost the same time you sit down—, looks boss as fuck. It's not hard if you frequent a place often and are friendly to the wait staff; plus it also takes little effort to develop a customer relationship with the waitresses in order to get them to remember you.

When I arrive in the suite— and they know what room type I like— there will always be a plate of fresh fruit waiting for me, as well as a bottle of wine and some miscellaneous snacks; roasted almonds, chestnuts, etc.

What you Need to know when you're Mobile

Like the foot soldier you are, you will often find yourself on the move during your stint in foreign lands; with respect to your side missions for your company. There's the 800 number for Joe Sixpack, and then there's the 800 number for Diamonds & Platinum's. That number, that 'you're-a-BigShot' number, should be saved into your device. You're more likely to get a human on the other end of the phone. Also, try to remain calm like a fucking Navy Seal. For whatever reason, people seem to think that *SCREAMING* at CSR's, threatening their jobs or whatever—like a middle-aged woman at a grocery store— will get them better results. You're *better* than that, we've *taught* you better than that, cadet. Screaming to get better results is seldom true and they may even simply annotate your PNR (Personal name record) as to what a raging dickhead you were, which isn't going to help you in the long run. Know-the-program and maneuver the CSR towards the resolution that you want. If you can't get it, you can always say *"Thanks for trying"*, click.

Hang up and call again. Remember what we talked about of Hyatt letting you use Cash & Points and suite upgrades, together. I know they do, because I've done this several times, but sometimes I get a CSR who swears I *can't*.

Lots of travel firms have a Twitter "ombudsmen" for lack of a better term. So, some traveler will tweet an issue to the company and evidently get it fixed almost immediately. Delta is known for this kind of service. It's still preferable to talk to a human being, I find at least. If you want something, ask for it. Higher-end hotels and increasingly mid-range ones will often send emails ahead of your stay, asking if there's anything they can do to make your stay more comfortable. The Woodlands, north of Houston, once famously fulfilled a couple's request (goofy I must add) for *three,* red fucking M&M's and a photograph of delicious bacon that they had put in the "special requests" box as a joke when making a reservation online. The point is, these higher-end hotel chains will go to extra lengths for you, no matter if you're trolling or not. If you want something, mention it. There are a couple of places I frequent where I specifically request extra towels and a bath robe along with other specific toiletries. Sometimes I will ask for certain beer to be stocked in the fridge or a cigar box to be put on the table.

Tipping

There is a way to be a badass with charm and class. So, for heaven's sake, 'service people' at the desk are people too. I tip bellboys around $5— this is for my 'rollaboard' and computer bag. If I have other bags, which I never do, that would increase a couple of bucks per bag. And yes *"In Europe, blah,blah,blah"* . I don't fucking care. Yes, be mindful that in certain areas of the world it is considered rude to tip (looking at you South Korea) and they will *actually* get offended. Whatever. Someday you're going to need a favor. I tip housekeeping $5 per day under ordinary circumstances. Bartenders and waiters I tip as normal. I don't tip desk staff except under extraordinary circumstances. For example, typically I have a very high tolerance for alcohol (and other various solvents).

One particular long haul, a young, attractive flight attendant took a liking to me and over-served me, as a result of my charm. Alcohol and high-altitude don't mix well: Although, if you like tomato juice, for whatever reason, it opens up nicely in the air for the flight attendants. Lufthansa did a study of what precise types of drinks they were handing out—evidently the Germans like to know these sorts of things— and it turns out that half of their non-alcoholic beverage requests were for tomato juice. So by the time I arrived at my hotel I was pretty fucked, to say the least.

So I tipped the girl at the front desk and I had a bellman show me to my room to make sure that I got there—it was one of those huge 'convention-type' hotels that one can get lost in fairly easily.

So, I tipped him double. He asked if there was anything I needed and I asked for a bottle of water—and joked about him calling Dr. Kevorkian to put me out of my misery. In California, they usually have water out as if it were candy. He disappeared to the supply room on the floor I was on and literally gave me an entire *case* of bottled water. At any rate, all was well that ended well, and when I checked back into that hotel three weeks later, they both remembered me fondly (half because I was a mess when they found me and because I tipped so well) because I wasn't a raging dickhead. If they were faking the fondness, who really fucking cares?; I had established a bond and relationship besides the fact.

The Doorman and Bellhop

Sure, they hold the door open for you and they may ball-hawk your bags for tips, but you have to be creative and think about how they can be valuable and an indispensible resource in other ways. Doorman and Bellhops are on the frontlines and know the comings and goings of everyone who is staying at the hotel. They provide the value of street-level Intel. If you decide one night to "order in", the doormen decide if the young lady (or ladies) get's past the door.

If I use a Bellman, I tip around $5 for my two bags. In non-U.S or Euro countries, if I don't have local currency handy, I use crisp (new) $5 bills. They're cool with it because money is money.

Concierge & Miscellaneous Desk Staff

The concierge is your Aide station. Need assistance with dinner reservations or theatre tickets and organizing day trips? He's your guy. Typically I don't need to use them, but when you're a rookie starting out you may need to rely on these people until you get the lay of the land, wherever you're being dispatched to. On a couple of occasions I've had them arrange for transportation—other than local taxis, which is handled by the doorman. Tip commensurate with serviced received, but I usually top off a concierge $10 or $20, more if warranted. Once upon a time I had a squad of friends who were stuck in the middle of the city with an impending snowstorm trying to get an EVAC home; with no luck as resources must had been tied up due to weather. They knew I frequently travelled there, so they reached out to me via phone. I had them vector-redirect to my hotel and go to the concierge at my favorite "Villa", who sorted them out with a special EVAC order with a tacit understanding that I would take care of him (the concierge) next time I saw him, which I did.

I was a *hero* to my friends and all it cost me was $30 and a phone call. The other front desk staff are there to greet you, competently check you in, validate your parking and break bills for you—and if they are female, smile and look pretty. At least, that's what I use them for.

House Keeping

The maids, the ones who make your bed and clean your bathroom when you're not there, are a vital service of course. Also, the "evening service" folks can come in handy as well if you need something in laundry or pressed. Take advantage of those services and feel more comfortable. One thing I do is send off whatever cloths I wore on those long haul flights to get washed and ironed. It just feels more civilized.

Sometimes, extras materialize. In a U.S hotel I stay in, a couple of coupons turned up from housekeeping, along with a thank you note. One was for 500 points in their rewards program and the other was for a free breakfast at the little cafe place they have—like a coffee and pastry joint. Now, the dollar value wasn't a big deal, but nice of them to make a gesture.

Having a Friend is a Great Thing

So at the Taj, where they were a bit forgetful about some things, they totally redeemed themselves by assisting me with another Taj. I was a frequent enough guest that I got to know some of the staff on a business level and the GM sent me an, *"If there is ever anything I can do for you...,"* Dear John type, email. Turns out, I was headed for London on "shore leave" and staying in a Taj property that was nice with a sweet price as well— just like everything else there, London hotels are fucking expensive and the bang-for-the-buck isn't always that great.

So, I pinged the GM the dates of my London travel and asked if he would do me a kindness (contact the GM at the hotel there) and mention that I was a frequent quest at Taj New York, and if he would extend every courtesy while I was in London. This turned out to be a *huge* win; as once I arrived in London, the red carpet and hookers (not quite... but you get my drift) came rolling out. Probably the best stay I've ever had there. All it took was an e-mail from the local GM—that I pretty much staged and scripted for him. Your goal here is to be "friendly" but not "BFF-y". Remember, your relationships in CorporateLand are all business.

Name Drop

What's the best thing you can do to help yourself when being a road warrior? Praise can be better than money sometimes. Every time I stay at a Hyatt property, I get an e-mail from Hyatt asking about my stay. Evidently, they actually read these *and* share them with staff because I've had them quoted back to me in follow-up thank you e-mails. So I have taken to writing out thoughtful responses and mentioning names. For example, I was trying, unsuccessfully, to "Shazam" a song at breakfast. One cute waitress who came over figured out what I was trying to do, and the next morning handed me a slip of paper with the song of the artist. I mentioned in my follow-up survey, and the next time I visited that hotel, she remembered and thanked me for it.

People in service industry positions who are there for the long haul are in it for a reason, an affirmation, especially when deserved, is not only pleasant for them, but useful as well. Once in a hotel in Toronto, I arrived late during the night, and there was a long ass hallway between the front desk and the elevators. There was a guy polishing the floor near the elevators. When he saw me and my entourage coming, he leaned over and pressed the "up" button to call the elevator to us. When the idea of 'customer service' has permeated all the way down to the guy manning the buffer on the graveyard shift you, as a hotel chain, are doing it right.

What if 'Villa Standards' have fallen & other issues Arise?

If there is a problem, I will *always* try to handle it with the local manager. It's better for them and more immediate results for you and me. Just like with a woman, maintain frame, and don't blow your cool like lunatic. You're like a ghost, and agent of sorts. You're cool is to remain calm, even if the world is being blown to smithereens around you. That's what a suit & briefcase should represent; this is what you've done to earn it. As an example, I was once staying at a Hyatt—where breakfast should have been free for me and up to three other squad members— staying in my room; such as a wife and kids if that's your shtick, or in my case, two 22 year-old women. The restaurant staff at the time seemed a bit confused over this. Not the girls; it's Europe, they get it—but they weren't registered to my room. Why? Because in the U.S, nobody would have bothered about it, but in Europe, they [hot ladies of the night] actually have to be registered guests. So I smoothed that over with the GM (he was a guy of course and understood), no problems. Technically though, I was wrong, but it was really more of a difference between how things are done in the U.S as opposed to how they are done in Europe. Once I registered them, order was restored to the Villa and everything was peachy.

Last time I was there, one of the girls at the front desk made a joke about the number (and identity) of women who might be staying with me at any given time—which was ok based on the nature of our relationship—and I said something along the lines of *"It depends on who is in town this week, and what their curfew is."* Laughs abound. If there is an issue with a room, or you just don't get all warm and fuzzy about it for some reason, ask for a different or better one. You're not being a raging dickhead, trust me. My last stay in Florida, I arrived late and there was some sort of group party with a shitty band that was so *fucking* loud I could hear it fourteen stories up. So I rang the front desk and asked to be moved across the hall to another side of the hotel, et volia! Problem, fucking solved.

Now, on the other hand, I know a guy who arrived late after being on a delayed flight and went to his hotel—this was in Illinois in the winter. The first room was akin to a broom closet, the second smelled like someone's grandparents died together in it and the third room had some weird temperature thing going on it it—freezing cold in one area, boiling Chinese Tea hot in another; that's how he described it. So finally, after the three disasters, a room finally opened up on the club floor. This was Illinois remember, in the winter, after midnight. Who were they possibly saving it for? Oprah? This also shows why you want to be in a program; he wasn't, but I suspect that even if he was just mid-tier there, it would have been enough to grease him through on the upgrade.

I had actually booked a room via the 800 line and the conversation got hung up on me because of my "audacious" demands. I was asking for a king sized bed for *three* people and the girl on the phone asked me if I needed a cot and I was all stuttering like *"nnnn, no, no, no cot."* She didn't understand. Eventually I said, *"Look, I have a 'Vicky, Christina, Barcelona' thing going on here. NO cot,"* and she sort of got it (sorta) but when I arrived, the # of guests on the reservation was 1, me. Fuck!

Cars

Let's all have a moment of silence first, for company cars. There...that's good enough. Like the apocryphal "key to the executive wash room", they just so rarely exist anymore in CorporateLand. I don't believe any corporation now has had such a thing as a 'car allowance' in the last fucking decade. These things only exist as "sense memories" now, of a better and distant time. Sort of how Democrats feel about the 60's and how Republicans feel about the 80's and maybe how Patrick Bateman probably felt about honey almond, body scrub. If I was sitting around a table with older guys, we'd all fondly reminisce about the boss who got us our first car; even if he was otherwise, a raging fucking dickhead. That said there are three ways cars factor into life in CorporateLand: Rentals, town cars, and Uber! For rentals, pick out a firm you like—I prefer Hertz—and get into their "#1 Gold" program or whatever Avis has, etc.

It's easy to do and you get better service and newer, lower mileage cars. In places where I rent frequently, it's nice to skip the line—we're going for *seamless* here people, and get rolling.

With town cars, if you're company *lets* you take town cars to the airport; fucking, *do it*. Does anything suck more than being stuck on the Van Wyck, when it's hotter than the devils asshole in July? Let someone else drive. Sure, it's a short trip, fuck it. Take your car if you want, but why? Better to ride in the air conditioned comfort of a town car. Chat with the diver if you want, or just chill out listening to Spotify—Rhapsody's sexy Swedish cousin. If I'm stepping off of a redeye, you'd better fucking believe there's a driver waiting for me; with a polished Lincoln or Caddy that still has that "new car" smell. Just like that eighteen-year-old who has that "new girlfriend" smell. Intoxicating, but might make you a little queasy after.

Pro Tip #1: Gratuity *will* be included, but an extra $10 is fine, if warranted. Not necessary, but always appreciated.

Pro Tip #2: Limo companies often have "rewards programs" such as: "Free airport transfer with every 10 rides". So, when I get to the free ride, I just use for *personal* travel.

Pro Tip # 3: Specifically "inside" pickup, rather than "curbside". It might be a few more beans for the guy to meet you at the baggage claim, but $10 is worth it to have him handle your luggage; getting off of a long haul flight and then wandering around outside Terminal 1 at YYZ (like a fucking idiot), looking for your driver in January, just sucks. It typically costs $10 more for the guy to meet you inside. If you can't find the guy, look near the baggage claim, because that's where he's going to expect you.

For example, in JFK International T4 there's an exit for people who don't have baggage to claim that's closer to the West Exit. When I can't locate my driver there, I know he is just on the other side near baggage claim.

Pro Tip#4: As for hotels, you can specify things as you want them. Want the local paper instead of the fucking New York Times? Not a problem. I specify temperature of the car. Limo companies clientele evidently trends older, so if you don't want the car's temperature set to "medium well" specify in the "Requests" section when making you rez. I tell them I want the car between 66 F and 68 degrees F. Drivers are usually men because they are more reliable, resourceful, and can honestly drive better.

Pro Tip #5: Be ready when the guy gets there if he's picking you up for an airport run. They usually show up 15 min early. I hand over my bag, tip the guy in advance, do one last look around of the house to see that the electronics and appliances are shut down etc., and we're underway 5-10 minutes after he arrives. They like leaving on time and so should you. If you delay them, after an interval (usually 30 min), you start to pay for the privilege.

Pro Tip #6: Depending on where you are, leave time for trouble and fucking around with traffic. I usually take all Thanksgiving week off, starting with the Friday before; same goes for any other holiday. If for some goddamn, fucking reason you have to travel on the Tuesday or Wednesday before T-Day, leave a shit ton of extra time for yourself. The last time I flew on one of those days, I gave myself 5 *fucking* hours— meaning I left my house 5 hours before my flight. The ride to the airport took more than double the usual time, but I was chilling in the airport club an hour before take-off, stress free, because of the LTT (Land Transfer Time) rule.

Uber

Uber got around to setting up some way of getting your expenses directly into Concur, which is popular expensive software. I had already set up my corporate card as a payment option, so I just e-mail the receipt to my admin. Uber has lost its initial "Wow" factor, now that everyone knows what the fuck Uber is; instead of assuming another German car company has formed. Back when it was new, I was out to dinner with a sales rep and a HUGE, IMPORTANT client— like tens of millions a year in revenue—and just as dinner ended it started to rain. Good fucking luck getting a taxi in NYC in the rain. Enter Uber, stage right. I think the multiple was 3.0x, but given the client revenue, the firm was 100% O.K with it and the client was amazed— as Arthur C. Clarke once said, *any sufficiently advanced technology is indistinguishable from magic.*

Restaurant *on* Lockdown Mode

LOCKING DOWN A RESTAURANT is important if you want to be a 'Big shot' at your firm or anywhere in CorporateLand. Lockdown Game can be hard but can be easier when the economy is a piece-of-fucking shit (which it has been in perpetuity). The best thing about a shitty economy is that the restaurant industry gets absolutely nailed in regards to foot traffic and ultimately hurts their bottom line. In times like these it is not only easier for you as a salesman, broker, manager etc., to lockdown a restaurant; but easier to lockdown the more prestigious ones. Back during the "Great Recession" high-end restaurants were begging for business like a pimpled faced teen on prom night for any sort of transaction to occur. So, times are tough still as they have been since 08'. What you need to do is pick a high-end restaurant or two; and no, not fucking AppleBee's, Michael Scott.

Do, of course, pick a place that you can bring multiple clients to. A place with fairly broad appeal: Steak, French, Italian, yes. Indian, Vegan, seafood [exclusivity], fuck no. A locally owned restaurant is probably going to be more open to our 'plan of action,' which I will get to in a minute.

Sometimes you can get a GM with a brain in his head, other times, not so much. Go in during non-busy hours, ask to speak to said GM. Introduce yourself, give him your card. Explain to him that you are in sales [or some other bullshit in CorporateLand] and that you often have to take your clients out to dinner. You can drive business to his place, but you want to feel comfortable there. If he is smart he will recognize the quid pro quo that is being communicated.

Ask for the following things: First, you want to be greeted by name by the Maitre D', without introduction. There should be no mistake by the Maitre D' of who you are. Second, you want to be shown to your table, immediately. It should be waiting for you. You know how you go into a place and they have that little "RESERVED for TOP DICKHEAD" sign on different tables? That's what *you* want. Indeed, they should be perfectly willing to let you choose your table, since you're there already. Third, you would like the chef to make a visit to your table during the meal. This may not always be possible, but if it's not too busy, and you're a VIP, they will make it happen.

Alternatively, they might suggest a kitchen tour, because it's easier for them. Other places will simply tell you to fuck right off, and well. You can either forgo that criteria, or pick another restaurant. The option of "Kitchen Tour" is fine if they agree to that. Most guys who take their clients out have been on more kitchens than care to, but sometimes you will have that client or customer who just absolutely *loves* that shit. So, you can work something out where they don't have to have a formal pre-scripted tour, just something on the spot. Clients won't know the difference. It's like giving a tour to school children at the Zoo; half the time the 'guide' just rolled-in after a night of drugs and Twenty-Something sex and just makes the shit up as they go.

The above criteria listed cost the restaurant *zero* dollars and at best, is a minor inconvenience. They should be happy to accommodate. If not, take your business and fun elsewhere.

Now for the fun stuff: Criteria involving Money!

Fifth, ask for a *discount* on wine. I'm fucking serious. This is Big-ball game now where the 'Big boys' play. If you think this is an unreasonable request to ask then you don't *belong* in CorporateLand; also if you know anything about economics and sales pricing you wouldn't judge me for a split second.

The mark-up on wine is fucking *enormous*, like 200-300% or more depending. Ask for 30% off; go down to 25% if you're a bit of a pussy, or if they start to haggle. If they get a bottle for $85 [the vineyard price on some very good pinot noir for sure] and sell it at $270 and you get $90 off, they still are making nearly double what they paid for it.

You may also ask for this favor when you come in on personal business with the wife/girlfriend/sidepiece /or out of town guests. This is total "*lockdown*" when you pull this off. What you choose to do on this is up to you and your own personal flare. The only real benefit is if you are trying to keep expenses down for your own benefit. If you can, meet the Sommelier and the Captain while you're meeting the GM of the restaurant. In fact, it isn't a horrible idea to ask to see the kitchen at the initial meeting; if you can meet the chef and/or sous-chef then, great.

This may all seem like overkill, but it's nice for people to be able to put a face to name, it goes along way, trust me. A word about the Som though— When you are at a restaurant and either are not familiar with the wine list or are in the mood for something new, ask to speak with the Som. Explain that you have $50 or $100 or $200 to spend on a bottle of wine that night and that you would like him to recommend something. If you have 'likes' or 'dislikes' let him know.

Don't be that prick. For example, you might say *"My price point tonight is around $150. I like Central Coast and Oregon pinot, but would be not be averse to trying a different varietal. I dislike Australian wine, however, but I do enjoy Tuscan reds, for example or things that have some heft but aren't so big that I have to eat them with a chain saw, like a big Cabernet."* You say something to that effect you not only look fuck'n money for saying it, you also give the Som some common courtesy and ability for them to do their job at selecting the best wine for your taste. People become Soms because they're really into wine and have a passion for it.

If you engage them in this way (in their language and show passion like they do) they will knock themselves out trying to get you the best bottle of wine at/near your price point, while using your parameters. It's like how you get a hard-on over a big sale you've made or a huge trade you closed on the Dow Jones that day; the Som blows his load when he finds that perfect wine for you and when you tell him what a great job he did in selecting said bottle. Be sure to tell him this if he does; as a man should receive full complements for doing his job well, whatever it may be.

Sixth, you can ask about being billed at the office on 7-14 days. It would be highly unusual for a restaurant to agree to this, but sometimes it's easier to give them one thing that they can say 'no' to for sure. One thing you want is to end the meal without your clients seeing the bill, or having it presented at the table. You can either make arrangements in advance, or simply get up after dessert/coffee has been ordered (not delivered) and excuse yourself. Take care of the bill while you're on your way to the Gents. It adds to the impression that you're a baller and the restaurant, your private club.

Seventh, do NOT cheap out on tipping. Most firms or institutions won't bat an eye at leaving a 20%'er. If you *can* get away with tipping more, do it. You're investing in the relationship you have with the restaurant. It's also ok to send the chef a brief note of thanks/compliment on the back of your business card. When you're out on your own and not using the company dime, tip with cash: Nothing say's "great job" like new and crisp, Yankee greenbacks.

Eighth, *your* job is to be a gracious host. The *restaurants* job is to help you do that. If anything goes wrong in this matter, address it as privately as possible and do not blow your cool like fucking drama queen. You're not a chick, are you? As an example, one night you may have a noob server at a high-end joint and her accidentally (because she's too busy staring at your lantern jaw and chiseled biceps) spilling wine on the table and maybe a bit on your shoes.

To most ballers this isn't a big deal, but it might be for *her* as it's not only embarrassing but may mean that she'd not receive a good tip that will ultimately subsidize her shoe-shopping, later. If it's not a big deal for you and the issue at hand not being DEFCON 1, then insist that the incident be <u>your</u> fault *"I accidentally turned my back and then brushed her arm when coming forward"* you'll say when the Captain swoops in to see what's all the commotion. It's not as if your suit needs dry-cleaning, it's just wine on the table and maybe on your hand.

Handle the matter with aplomb. More than likely you will see this same waitress down the road, when's she's moved up the ranks and she will most likely never fail to visit your table[if you're not already in her section], greet you by name, and extend courtesies towards you. Most guy's will be intolerable assholes to these women so being a gentlemen in this setting and regard will actually work to your benefit as you will stand out. I know, it's ironic, but this isn't a night club or a bar where being the guy who's a slight dickhead will get you laid vs. 'nice guys' buying the girls drinks all night. This is a waitress in a *WORK* setting, it's a different dynamic. Trust me, they remember shit like this and how you handled the situation with them; they will forever remember you for it. Sparing them of embarrassment and maybe even losing their job or hours, depending on how their boss views the fuck-up. It never hurts to have a friend....toward that end.

Ninth, if warranted, review the restaurant *online*. Why? The food and service warrant it and for that reason only. It also buys a shit-ton of good will. Email copies to the Maitre D's that you deal with and I *shit you not* they will actually read these out load at their staff meetings. Write it well too. They want to tell their staff this sort of shit and say to all of them, *"See, this is how people should feel after they eat here"*. The review will cost you nothing beyond the time it took to compose[less than one hour, and on company time of course] and you better believe that the red carpet will come rolling out the next time you go to your restaurant(s) that you now have on "Lockdown".

How to Taste Wine

The bit where you taste the wine is theater. You're really checking to see if the wine is corked or otherwise not in proper condition. This rarely happens these days, but it is still possible, when natural cork is used; a bottle with a screw-top or a synthetic cork *cannot* be 'corked'. It may have other problems from improper storage, but it won't be corked. So, does you wine have an 'eau due musky grave with notes of wet dog fart about it? Then it's corked.

Not likely, but possible. If this happens to you, put the glass down and ask the Som to taste it. He will pour himself a bit and investigate. If it's really corked the restaurant should have no problems making amends. Onward.

The wine will be brought to the table and presented. Make sure that it matches what you ordered. Mistakes are rare, but it's possible. When you're ordering, it's also perfectly fine to include the bin number, as in, *"Let's start with the Moulin Rouge, 2007* [If they have more than one vintage], *bin #8567"* It's not necessary, but they won't toss you out for it and it makes it easier for them. It's good to do this, particularly for the French wines if you have pronunciation that will someday land you in Language Jail in Paris, for Crimes Against The French Language. Once the wine has been presented, assuming it is the correct bottle, simply nod your head like a Gambino giving the 'yes' to a hit on a mark, or ask them to pour it for you if you're feeling extra rich. The cork will be removed and placed on the table. Leave it where it is. Feel free to crack the joke about how you're tempted to screw the cork into your ear and say, *"Sounds good, pour it"*. Most at your table will laugh because they most likely will have never heard that one before.

The Som and the waiter will laugh because, well, they pretty much have to. The Som will pour a small amount of wine into your tasting glass. Swirl it gently like your some type of royalty so that the wine swirls around the glass no higher than half way. You can do this by holding the stem or by using your hand on the base; like the way your girlfriend holds your balls when she's greasing your gator.

You primary goal is to keep the wine in the glass from splashing out; unlike your girlfriends goal of trying to get your vinaigrette out of your skin-tube. Your secondary goal is to aerate it a bit and see how it will taste when it opens up; the same way your girlfriend finds out after you air drop your stuff after she opens wide. The lines that trail down the glass, those are called "legs" or "tears" (the analogies write themselves). They used to be deemed important to some, but really it's a function of the alcohol content [or viscosity] of the wine, and it has nothing to do with quality, but if one of your clients thinks otherwise, don't ruin the illusion for them; you and the Som can laugh, privately, about it later. Next, smell the wine. Get your cheese-cutter schnoz deep in the glass and take a good subterranean, long whiff, but only one. First, you are seeing if it's corked. Second, as smell and taste are closely related, you are gathering information about the wine.

Take the wine into your mouth as if it were your first encounter with new, lush, feminine lips. Don't gulp it down like the town booze hound; you're *not* at Hooters. Some people will draw air into their mouths and the sound will be similar to someone getting that last bit of soda or shake out with their straw. Again, this is to see how the wine tastes when it has been opened. Get a sense of the 'heft' the wine has. Lastly, swallow. Hold for a second. That's the wine's "finish" or aftertaste. If the wine is acceptable, ask the Som to pour it.

When can you send the wine back?

Every guy in CorporateLand will have their own rule or qualm about this. A good rule is if there is something *actually* wrong with the wine (i.e. corked, improperly stored, otherwise damaged, sending it back should not be an issue). Now, if you plain just don't like the wine? Hmm, you may have a problem, Houston. If you fuck up, that should be on you. This is why you should scout the wine list first in advance. Why? If it's a business dinner, you want it to go smoothly and you want to stack the line-up with winners (aka Your Old friends). Your 'Old Friends' are the wines that you know for sure are winners.

A few other notes: Some places will have a 'reserve list'. This is the "Swinging, Big Boy Dick" wine list. It's going to [or should] have excellent wines on it. They are going to be costlier than what is on the basic list, naturally. If there is a reserve list and you know about it and your guests don't, casually ask to see it— that is a classic, smooth jazz move, my friend. That will make your clients/guests feel all warm and special; and people who feel warm and special like being around you and they also like *buying* from you.

What if there is someone more experienced with wine at the table? Don't be afraid to ask their opinion and step aside. Stepping aside when another man has more experience is a classy move and it would be worse to try and upstage him when they have a .50 cal Desert Eagle knowledge about wine and you a .22 or even a 9mm or .45 cal. Respect the wisdom, respect the knowledge, and respect the *size* at the table. It will be beneficial not only for you but for everyone else who's just as interested in learning this shit. If you remain classy, about little shit like this, it goes along way. It can pay dividends down the road in clients actually inviting *you* out to dinner, to lay the lumber down on the wine list.

Also, clients or customers over 40-45, especially the long haul marrieds, will want to hear about your travels to exotic locations and you banging women half their age; so they can daydream later, about being half as cool as you. You=*Puts on Wayfarers*. More seriously though, if there's someone at the table more experienced than you, it's always *ok* to include them; you won't lose Alpha points on this one because the information will most likely be beneficial to save in your own vault and arsenal of knowledge. For example, you may've dined with some dude who knew better when it came to French reds. Guess who now chooses French reds when you two go out? Exactly. If that guy is at the table, he's in charge of France, and you can be in charge of Italy and California. It's a great way to learn about wines outside of your neighborhood.

Lastly, wine tasting is more art than science. It's about the experience. *"Black currant, red cherries, forest floor...with notes of toasty oak"* If your wine glass has pine needles in it, fucking send it back to be strained. Great wine is meant to be shared, and properly deployed it can help build camaraderie and relationships. CorporateLand isn't all full of douchbags and raging dickheads. You *can* find some guys who are actually worth hanging out with, learning from, going to dinner and talking shop. It's what you make it and how you approach each relationship.

The Female Social Matrix

MEN ARE NORMALLY the ones accused of misogyny...but honestly, we're amateurs at the art when being compared to women who are *masters* at it. Don't believe me? Have you ever heard a woman/girlfriend come home after a day at her job and *not* complain or bitch about her other female co-workers? Yeah, thought so. The Female Social Matrix is omnipresent. From its humble origins at church socials and various sorts of "bees", though it's maturation in the 1960's at Tupperware parties, to its full-fledged entry into the workforce in the 70's and 80's, the FSM is everywhere. Nowhere is it stronger or more important to understand than in the corporate world. Feminism evolved conceptually, largely in response to the need for adapting domestic female culture to the predominantly-male, rugged, and cut-throat business world.

With its emphasis on quality and sisterhood, feminism—Equity feminism, mind you—was before SJW's and Gender Feminism were ~~born~~ miscarried yet survived in zombie-like fashion and declared a holy war on all things 'male'. True feminism, and the one that is most noble and practical, was supposed to be about women helping women compete in a man's world. Since around that time of adoption, that's been a slow but inevitable process; the workforce went "co-ed", and the emphasis went from being on a woman's right to work and receive a fair and equitable wage to the lack of female managers and CEO's running CorporateLand.

The fabled Glass Ceiling, beyond which all wishes of power, fortune and influence, would supposedly be granted. Special mentoring programs and other remedial resources were thrown at the problem—feminism couldn't very well argue for the right of every woman to be free-to-work and establish her own financial independence without taking exception to the lack of boobs in the conference room. Then, special regulations, dealing with issues of sex and sexuality came along—which had to be developed for use, so terms like "boobs in the boardroom" would be legally actionable in the wrong context. Women demanded the right to compete, and then changed the rules of competition (watering them down) in business to favor themselves.

This is where we are today in CorporateLand, education, military etc, where everything has been padded and made 'Child Safe for Use' so that women can "fairly" compete with men. They are not competing with men on a man's level; they are competing with themselves on their level—while men still have to put out at a maximum. Hence, why you still don't see many female CEO's and managers—women get a trophy for just showing up and they seem to be O.K with that. So, for over 30 years, more than an entire generation, we've seen women at work, some women in management, women "competing in a man's world"(we use that phrase *very* loosely) even though the "man's world" is looking more feminine than ever.

That's the only way women can compete and survive in today's world; everything needs to be watered down or else they fail completely, and we can't have any tears now can we? The result isn't pretty, and it turns out that this utopia that feminists have mapped out isn't paying dividends for women and is in fact making their lives worse. When men self-organize, they usually do it in hierarchal fashion, with clear top-down leadership, management and execution. Things work out great this way. There is a central power and then subordinates who comply execute the leadership's policies and decisions. It's all very *impersonal* and extremely ***effective*** for that reason.

Building a wall, house, ship, or civilization for the matter, or defending your genetic destiny from a hostile world...you know *important* things. Male-dominated organizations traditionally emphasize the archaic qualities of achievement and competition, depending on mere efficiency, innovation, and ingenuity to get by.

Women, on the other hand, self-organize in a *far* more **_unsophisticated_** way. Unfortunately for them, the self-organization of the Female Social Matrix *punishes* achievement and emphasizes co-operation and fairness over efficiency or efficacy. However, that *doesn't* mean that it's not competitive. On the contrary, it is, but just in a different and unproductive way when relating to the business world (aka unnecessary competition/petty competition). Regardless of how many women are in a workplace, more than one leads to a node for the Matrix to exist. Despite how many men work with these women, the FSM is ALWAYS overlaying the organization.

Life in the Crab Basket isn't great for women in CorporateLand. If you're on the bottom, every other crab is stepping on you, constantly shifting in unpredictable ways, making any progress difficult because crabs *aren't* organized. If you're in the middle, not only is your foundation constantly moving, everyone around you is attempting to climb over you to get closer to the top of the basket; the crabs at the top of the basket who are using you as support are just as eager to keep their position and discourage ambitious competition.

There's just only so much room up at the very top of the basket and *everyone* wants to be there. So the vaunted "cooperation" slogan that women and feminists love to tout as an advantage of female-led enterprises turns instead into a series of insurmountable, petty competitions. None of which are decisive but all of which add to the general instability of the basket. It's all by *design*.

Let's be honest, it is very difficult to rise to the top of the basket without the help of the crabs on your level, and those below you. Eventually, you have to step on some crabs. When you are all striving for the same goal, the same thing that everyone wants (which is inherently limited) then competition, **not** cooperation, actually rules the day. For women in the office, the crabs on their level aren't their "sistas", they're bitches and cockroaches that need to be squashed who are in the way. If a woman isn't standing on another's shoulders one day, looking down, then others will be standing on theirs. The crabs on the top or the 'Queen Bees' are the ones who have successfully completed the race to #1 , which means they now have to *constantly defend* their position. Leadership and power in the FSM is *always* transitory. *Everyone* gets a turn on the town bicycle, so to speak. Of course, there's only room for one ass on the seat at a time...however every crab thinks it should be their ass, and none feel more entitled to that seat then the ones that are already sitting on the bicycle.

Female managers suck, if you're a female employee. Queen Bees regularly sabotage those crabs and drones below them who look most challenging and threatening to their position. While talking about leveling the playing fields and bridging gaps and providing opportunities:

When women gain power their first impulse is to secure their position by eliminating competition as savagely and ruthlessly as possible...without looking like they're really doing it. While that worked out great back in the 17th century for the quilting and knitting bee, when that method of social organization is applied to the masculine-developed world of CorporateLand, the FSM imposes some harsh problems on women in the workplace. Men have nothing to do with it. Men aren't competing with women here because they are honestly not the threat, its other men who are trying to pull rank. Women are too busy fighting with each other that they *never* even make it to the level where men are at. It's the sad reality, but it's true and this is the main reason why men dominate in CorporateLand, still. So, how come women insist that they are better at "cooperating" and getting along as a group than men? It's because that very fiction is a powerful strategy in the Crab Basket. Remember, a lot of the times women will self-project their own agenda and strategies to you. By women convincing other women that they're all 'good companions' rowing down the river together, it creates a false environment; an environment ripe for backstabbing.

If all women believe that their female colleagues aren't out to get them and that it's the Man who is, or their male co-workers, than it's ever the more easier for them to initiate a surprise attack or "drive-by" on their main competition: other women. That's why women shouldn't compare themselves to men when in CorporateLand, because they never even make it to the octagon with them. Women would be better off comparing and fighting for 'top stop' in more female dominated institutions such as education, or Single-mommyLand. Saying that there is a Glass Ceiling in CorporateLand is a complete waste of words because the women here can't even make it to the ladder to get anywhere near Elysium. By insisting that everyone is equal, even the men, and that the Basket should strive for fairness—an ideal world in which *everyone* gets to be on top of the basket and nobody has to be on the bottom, that allows for the rationalization the more ambitious crabs need to sabotage their comrades' progress under the slightest pretext. It's classic Socialist and Marxist thinking at its finest to be honest. Since they, too, have to agree to the polite fiction of female cooperation—in order for their competitive nature to thrive—they cannot do so, openly; or risk the wrath of the rest of the basket. The offence and trample is *always* personal with the ladies too (no matter how much they assure you it isn't).

Where in men accept defeat to another man, who is clearly savvier in his skill set (and most often deserving), women hold an unnecessary grudge when at the end of the day, business is just that: business. Being emotional in CorporateLand will get you killed. Keeping your head on straight and working to perfect your craft will most often lead to better things.Becoming emotional and taking everything as a personal offence will cause you to lose focus, lose your stride and ultimately sabotage yourself; if someone else hasn't already done it to you. Women are emotion, thus seem to have panache for unwittingly providing the rope to hang their self with. Indeed, women in CorporateLand are *constantly* turning work-related issues and relationships, *personal*.

This is most likely because the female dual cooperation/competition dichotomy encourages a *personal*, rather than *impersonal*, style of behavior. The FSM is inherently personal and inherently judgmental, and when those two elements are mixed with business or other enterprise...it can get ugly. Women, it turns out, aren't very good *employees*, either. An ambitious, hard-working corporate female doesn't see female leadership above her as a potential ally, but as a natural and eventual foe. Undermining the success of the Queen Bees of an organization covertly, through manipulating the Matrix, is a time-honored method of advancement amongst women.

This is mostly done on a social level and not through the normal male metric of achievement and demonstration. In the Basket or HoneyHive, it doesn't matter how well Stacy is at her job, *it matters what everyone thinks of her*. Female managers have it rough though, because not only do they have to deal with the male-oriented demands of the business world and lead accordingly, they have to concurrently manage their own shit Basket of women and keep the latter from screwing them up the ass with the effectiveness of the former.

On the other hand, that happens so often it's ironic here. As female managers deal with countless, petty personal attacks on their leadership in the form of constant gossip among their female co-workers and other subordinates, they also have to contend with a far different range of expectations from their female employees than their male employees. On the whole, female managers would perhaps rather have male subordinates than female, since male demands in the workplace are far less and more practical. Females tend to want to make life hard for managers since they only want to work something like 3 days a week and also book off time as if they were big shot CEO's, only that they aren't; they're subordinates. A female manager's male employees, for the most part, stick to the male-hierarchical business model regardless of who is in charge and are actually more likely to treat a female boss impartially and objectively, looking at her performance and leadership before allowing their personal feelings to enter into their judgment.

However, the Crab Basket is a vicious place. Her female subordinates will often be brutal critics—not of her performance as a leader, but of her *personal* life and use that as the basis of their level of cooperation. Often women in a subordinate role to other women—particularly younger women—will often inspire a "mothering" reflex in them. This in itself leads to a lot of instability when the goal is not to find your boss a husband, but to do your job and make the company money. It's also very difficult for an older woman to take orders from a younger woman without giving guff about it; and second guessing her younger boss constantly. I've seen some older women actually take their younger superiors to task over their performance and decision-making in an effort to "help" them.

That is the key to the Crab Basket model, thought: When all of those women are tugging and pulling you back down to their misery, they aren't being malicious...they genuinely think that they are "helping" you; at least, that is what they tell themselves. When a woman gains accolades or achievement that singles her out amongst the herd—sends her to the top of the basket— then the FSM prohibits *open* activity against her, because it violates the Matrix's rules. Direct confrontation is an affront to the dignity of femininity, or something like that. Any attack must be cloaked in some sort of ruse or guise. You can't go after another woman directly without appearing to be a Bitch (which is something of a mixed blessing in CorporateLand).

Instead, they hover around like hyenas, waiting for the ascending crab to make a *crucial mistake*...and then they will all descend on her, not to "attack" her, but to *"help out"*. More high-achieving women have been "helped out" of their success by their ostensibly well-meaning rivals or subordinates than by sexist male bosses. That, you can take to the bank. Most women know this instinctively, thanks to their multi-track communication modes. When a man hears, *"Would it be helpful if I came over and gave you hand around the house?"* from his sister-in-law, to him it's a friendly offer and is taken literally as a good faith gesture. To his wife though, it's a tacit condemnation on her skills as a wife and mother. This shit is serious, young trainee, *really*.

It's serious because this affects everything from your work environment, home, buddies who have GF's or wives, all the way to your own sex life and the women that you "see". Understanding even this one concept can change the way you operate for the better in all aspects of your life.

This facet of the Crab Basket has to be seen in light of the Hamster Wheel of collective femininity. Essentially, the "Bless her Heart" motivation is the *rationalization of competitive behavior as assistance, with compassion during crisis* being placed at the highest level of female values. Everyone is all sista-sista and BFF's when the basket is stable...until a crab shows any weakness. That weakness is an opportunity to strike, while gaining Matrix points for the overt demonstration of a "helping hand".

Another example: Ms. CrabApple is the head of her department and is killing it this fiscal period; she's doing very, very well. Her numbers are up from previous years and her employees are motivated. She's making good decisions and getting noticed by those Big Wigs higher up; in good ways *and* in bad ways. The more she rises, the more she comes under scrutiny and criticism over her personal life—which everyone in the Matrix seems to (or claims to) know all about. As long as she doesn't fuck up, the crabs have to keep their claws under the covers.

Suddenly, however, Ms CrabApple's mother get's an illness and needs a major surgery. She thus has to take time off of work to take care of her. She then files for FMLA and takes a leave for the purpose, assured that she will have a job when she gets back from dealing with the crisis. In the meantime, she does what she can to prepare for her absence. If she's any good, she'll probably be able to delegate enough to subordinates, post-pone non-essentials, and monitor affairs from a remote location if necessary, to put out any fires if they should come to life. It's a hassle, it's a pain in the ass, but it's necessary and Ms. CrabApple can handle it. However, the moment the scent of crisis is loose upon the Matrix, Ms. CrabApple's "need" for compassion turns into an opportunity to exploit weakness; By "helping" her, to *death*.

Her female boss (who has been growing more and more threatened by Ms. CrabApples's rising abilities) moves into her position for the interim and assumes an executive role in the time of crisis. She assures Ms.CrabApple that things will be *just fine* in her absence because *everyone cares so deeply* about her and what she is going through in her time of "need". Open displays of sympathy are on parade, breaking normal work protocol: Card's, flowers, even Fund Raising. The agitation that the Matrix can generate around the "wounded" member; equals the more points available for everyone. Then the deeply sympathetic boss completely reorganizes Ms. CrabApple's department and workflow to "help her" become more efficient. That is, run more to *her* liking. She'll appear matronly and concerned to the rest of the employees, which preserves her position in the FSM— shit, it improves it! Bestowing compassion is an automatic 100 points. Compassion in a leadership position, fuck'n doubles it. You're probably wondering by now, *"Does it stop here, sir?"* Negative, private. Ms. CrabApple's boss is just get'n started.

The Matrix is ubiquitous as we've learned in our research here in CorporateLand and the weakness is an opportunity for everyone involved. Ms. CrabApple's female subordinates take advantage of her absence to advance themselves shamelessly, "helping out" Ms. CrabApple by taking away her cherished projects, key client relationships or plumb assignments.

They'll all sign a card and chip in ten dollars, too, just for the cheap and easy Matrix points. Remember, Generosity in a Time of Crisis is a cool, mint, 200 points; they'll simultaneously begin sabotaging Ms. CrabApple's efforts subtly, working through the Matrix gossip and speculation, *"Did you see how haggard she's looking these days? She's aged ten years since March! Bless her heart though because she loves her Mama. And did you say she only offered you 10%? Mr. Pear, I can go fifteen...I have no idea why she would treat you like that. Must be the stress."* And her actual rivals? If she does indeed have an enemy, then this crisis is blood in the water for the shark. Sometimes a very calculated bit of "help" will be used to force Ms.CrabApple into a favorable position—Says Ms. DragonFruit, her rival in another department, as she generously offers the use of her peaceful mountain cabin for her mother's recuperation, free of charge...and doesn't bother to mention that there is no Wifi or cell-phone coverage. While Ms.CrabApple is soaking up the rustic vibes of the mountain range and tending to her mother, Ms. DrangonFruit is systematically raiding her files, poisoning the waters against her, and preparing booby-traps like the Vietcong for her eventual return. Even her female allies will accidentally work against her, in the name of "helping her". Phone calls, texts and emails keeping her apprised of the corporate Matrix re-positioning, can call even more attention to her.

Attempts to defend her land by her loyalist guards can result in even further loss of power and position, and can thus endanger their own positions. When a coup d'etat is trying to form in the office, suddenly everyone's position of power is in danger.

Of course, by the time Ms. CrabApple returns, her mom might be better, but her career is ultimately screwed. A soft coup has taken place in her department and she now has to try and regain her power. The law says she has to come back to a job, but it doesn't say it has to be her old job. She could even wind up as assistant to her former subordinate, *"You were gone so long, we just couldn't be without a leader for that long..."* and subordinate to her former rival will say, *"Janice knew it would take you a while to get back up to speed..I'm sure this is temporary, until you've recovered"* and be safely neutralized as a threat to her former boss.

A coup is hard to spot in the office if you're a rookie because everyone is just *oozing* with sympathy and compassion, worry, and concern. Did you see that card there? *Everyone* signed it. With that said, these are the very signals and signs to which make up a coups success in CorporateLand. And holy hell, God help her, if she becomes entangled with a man— or even rumor of one— while she's gone. Don't kid yourself, one little ounce of, *"I thought I saw her the other day at a restaurant when she was supposed to be taking her mother to the doctor...and you should have seen the guy she was with!"* Nail in the coffin.

If that's whispered in the break room at noon, while everyone is taking out their ham & cheese, it's all over. Mere speculation of her personal life, with a caked-in opportunity for judgment and loss of position, is when the claws get sharpened under the table. It doesn't have to be true; it just has to *appear* to be the truth, or true enough to sound good to the women in Accounting. Concern becomes an opportunity for judgment and criticism. And it's always personal.

While all of this is taking place, the men in the office are largely clueless or impotent. They fight a different kind of war in the office and neither have the tools or expertise on how to deal with this level of Matrix activity. For men, it's the equivalent of fighting a guerilla war from the air. All they see is a lot of whispering, cards and flowers, posturing, and a lot of speculation on what might happen to Ms. CrabApple. Any attempt by a male to dissuade the women from going after Ms.CrabApple's position will result in a unified response and front from the corporate United Matrix Alliance, chastising him for his lack of compassion—*can't he see that everyone only wants what is best for Ms. CrabApple, that they love her so?* Female rivals, allies, subordinates, and superiors will all insist that they are acting out of a sense of "love" and "compassion" while they effectively hamstring Ms CrabApple's position.

It gives all of them the camouflage they need to pull off such a military operation in plain sight of their target. Every crab in the basket is insisting that they are helping Ms. CrabApple as she gets pushed lower down the Basket. If you're a dude and you know what's actually going on, it can be horrifying to watch. It's the difference between, *"Is there anything I can do to help?"* and *"LET me help you...no really, I insist!"* So, next time you see some up-and-coming shining example of female success about to storm the glass ceiling and take the job you covet, pay attention to just how quickly her fortunes turn around through indirect attacks and social manipulation when she's going through a "rough patch". As a dude, you're actually pretty lucky. You don't have to lift a finger, open the book with the nuclear codes, or even press the button; the Matrix will take care of her for you. Each day that passes as she's trying to get closer to your position of power, means more enemies will gather behind her, trying to take her down along the way. The hill for her seems to get steeper with each passing sunset.

The collective weight of the Hamster Wheels will flatten a female rival for you as a man far quicker than mere out-production. Oh, and if you're a Black Knight, you can bloody the shark invested waters with a little disinformation mumbled into the right ear, to either hurt or help her *("Cancer? Funny, I heard she was interviewing for a Director-level position with our largest competitor,"* is one that can throw the Matrix into a hail storm, for example).

While it is generally ungentlemanly and un-classy to bring up a personal issue when competing with a rival, don't forget that Ms. CrabApple, or any woman for that matter, would not hesitate mentioning that she saw your Mustang in the parking lot of a strip club to your female boss, if she has the chance. If you want to pile onto the Crab Basket with your weight, understand that as a male you are not part of the Matrix, but that doesn't mean you can't influence it since it is a living breathing thing. You just have to know how to properly shake the Crab Basket. The simplest way is to casually mention something *intensely* personal but still *vague* enough for masculine plausible deniability.

The fact that you're a dude, and you don't even really understand the Matrix, gives you standing as an *information source*. You have some level of credibility just because everyone in the Matrix knows you don't know shit about the rules of the Matrix (but now you do), so why would your merely-male ass lie to them? Hamsters supply all the details you need. So, if you really want to fuck with Ms. CrabApple and her career, the quickest and most direct way is to casually mention a potential indiscretion of hers to pretty much *anyone* in the Matrix.

Mention, just once, how you saw her flirt with a married dude to the "wrong" node in the Matrix (a node that seeds signals to all other components), and she's *toast*. No one in the FSM likes a woman who will flirt with another woman's husband, even if they do so regularly on their own. Unless Ms.CrabApple is a confirmed lesbian, that's all the rationalization the FSM needs to tear her apart. So be aware of the hazards the Crab Basket represents, regardless of your gender and skill-set. You can't avoid it. It's how things are; no matter how many feminist rants and sisterhood chants you hear. Watch what they do, not as they say.

This is war remember. In war, how you win depends on how committed you are to the cause; you need to *want* it more than your opponent, which means you have to do the extreme and immoral thing most times. War isn't for pussies. It's to get pussy in the end by way of power, control and money; all things to which CorporateLand represents and has been built on.

The Male Social Matrix

THE MALE SOCIAL MATRIX is a lot more straightforward and easier to explain since it is not built from passive-aggressive nodes and fluidity. It has to be addressed, nonetheless, since men will be the tougher competition in CorporateLand and actually require you to do more with the skills you have (knowledge) than just letting women sabotage themselves in the office. Men, when they congregate in male-only groups, quickly establish a soft, somewhat flexible dominance hierarchy almost immediately; through subtle gestures, body postures, gentle discussion, and *demonstrations of intelligence* and worthiness based on the unwritten/oft-written about code of masculine behavior. Men value respect and from respect, drive authority.

Watch how a group of men who are total strangers to each other act when they meet, say at a wedding, funeral, or civil ceremony. The basic ritual is the same, whether it's a group of teens or a bunch of grave-callers. You as a man size up the other members of the group first, and use visual cues to determine status. The obvious signs are taken into account: Does that man wear a watch? If so, what kind, and what does that say about his personality and character?

Is he dressed appropriately for the situation? If not, why the fuck not? Is he carrying a cane or a weapon?—A briefcase, or an umbrella, his wife's purse? All of these will tell you where he fits into the greater social scheme. However, that is the cursory inspection. Men, unlike women, value *character* over *context* in a social situation. Which make women the truly shallower sex and most petty. Men care about how firm the other's handshake was. Did he address you by name? Did he get your title right? Does he act like he has his shit together? Is he an obvious, dickbag? All of these elements go into male assessment of other men in small groups. Men, in other words, prefer to establish a "pecking order", an informal or formal hierarchical structure which provides a *stable* and transitive order and chain of command—unlike the female Crab Basket, which has no order.

If there's a group of four-high powered executives in suits and an unemployed, unshaven dude in casual wear sitting at a table, for example, a woman would see four Alpha's and a rumpled Gamma based on their appearance. Four winners (assuming they aren't faking it) and a loser. However, the men who quickly established that the unemployed man was in fact the *most* Alpha, being recently medically discharged from the Special Forces for injuries received while leading a platoon of men into an Afghanistan Operation, **invested in the unemployed soldier with the bulk of their respect and admiration;** thus, making him a temporary Alpha of the group.

Respect and admiration for personal character, as exemplified by the masculine ideals of courage, sacrifice, honor and bravery, trumped their mere material success. Regardless of the job titles of the executives or their salaries, they would forever be inferior to the man who took up a rifle, shot a bunch of no good fucking terrorist pieces-of-shit(in the fucking *face* mind you), and risked his life to preserve his lot and that of his comrades on the battlefield. Being in the presence of a man, who probably turned some Muhammad's chest into a cavity of pulpy chutney— ruining his Allah's Snack Bar with a M26 frag— deserves respect. God I fucking hate those pieces of shit terrorist, camel jockeys. I wish they could just turn that whole region into radiated parking lot. Shit stain of the world I tell ya. Waste of space. I digress.

Anyway, men tend to form their own social hierarchies based on a fairly limited but firm criteria, and we do it, very, *very* quickly (because we are that good). We do it so well because it makes sense, it's logical and it's of course bred into our hardwiring. It's the best method we have as men, hence, why civilization was created. You're welcome, ladies. We like rules and laws because, well, the universe has rules and laws. Remember, one of the first things the Lord of the Flies boys did when they made it to the island was start making up *"Rules! We have to have lots of rules!"* We make rules because we as men know how bad other people can be. It's for our own protection.

Men like firm social boundaries, standard metrics of success and failure, validation and condemnation in easy-to-chew, bite sized pieces. We like to know that if we do well by an *objective* measure we will progress. Basically, men like to know the rules, cost-benefits, and risks of the game before we play; which is smart because it's not impulsive or based on emotion (which can sabotage you). Nor is the first "Alpha" necessarily set in stone. As the size of the group increases, sub-groups will naturally form around strong individuals. That's expected and accepted, because competition is one of our natural male elements. We *want* to see the Alphas fight it out— with the one with the best ideas or most persuasive arguments taking the unofficial "Alpha guru" title; until a better leader comes along.

While men form hierarchical organizations very quickly, they are also prone to allowing their order to decrease over time, allowing demonstrably more competent leadership to take the field.

If the purpose of the group is purely a social one, then that happens in conversation. We start bragging, shooting the shit, telling stories that refer to our achievements and accomplishments, establishing a masculine type "street cred" with a history of how we've survived these parts. Or, we use the opportunity to demonstrate our wit and humor, a demonstration of intelligence and character. Possibly we will show off trophies that exemplify our success, our tastes, our achievements, or our wealth. In this setting, every male is theoretically in play for the Alpha card and if there is alcohol involved then things may well proceed to Demonstrations of Worthiness, including dangerous testosterone-laden stunts involving fire and farts. It's all *very* manly. If the purpose of the group is practical, with a goal or a mission in mind, then the males self-organize behind the Alpha best able to command their loyalty and respect by his presentation. They will often give him their respect and loyalty in good faith straight up, particularly if he has the initial social status to command it.

However, once the mission starts, that respect and loyalty is *conditional* on his performance. This can be seen in CorporateLand all the time with account managers losing their clients (thus ultimately losing their account) and the changing of the guard when a leader can't make the quarters shine as brightly as last year's bulbs on the tree. It's nothing personal, it's just business.

Losing the confidence of the men saps the leader of the respect upon which his authority is based. They will often give him the opportunity to re-claim it, but repeated failures will provide an opportunity for a secondary Alpha being unofficially elected as leader, the respect and power of authority is thus transferred to the new leader. In male groups, initial social position is no guarantee of respect and admiration. Watch a group of men from a company go to Habitat for Humanity and build a house, for example. Once the cuff-links, ties, suits, and vodka breath come off and there are hammers and nails in their hands, the measure of respect is your competence, not your title. Bob who's your superior, a guru at managing accounts, may not be the best at making a shelf for the little Honduran kids to put their non-existent books on. When you are building a wall, or pouring concrete, it doesn't matter if you have a MBA, that social context is now meaningless against the ability to drive a nail into some wood.

Because of the mission and mission parameters, the male social hierarchy ideally re-arranges to put those demonstrating the best competence in a leadership position. This is why men progress and do so well in groups of other men (hence why we have civilization) because in any scenario, the best man for the job (even if he wasn't the Alpha before) will be chosen and the rank and file will be re-shuffled; so that he (the chosen Alpha for that particular situation) can be allowed to take the reins for the greater good of the group, and more importantly for the greater good of society.

A good Alpha with social skills will accept his demotion gracefully and with good humor, transferring his respect and therefore his authority to the new Alpha. A poor Alpha resents his temporary displacement and resentment will reflect poorly on his character. Men are pretty easy: **Competence, respect, admiration, authority, loyalty, success.** That's how you become top dog in the office as man. The success of the group is a larger factor than the success of any particular individual, but the failure of the group is ultimately the responsibility of the Alpha leader. When the group succeeds, then the subordinates are granted respect and admiration by the Alpha leader. When the group fails, the Alpha leader should blame, for the most part, himself and acknowledge his defeat personally; as General Lee did after the Civil War.

Groups like team sports, the military, Boy Scouts, and naval culture are all based upon the masculine model of social organization. The focus is the mission, and devotion to that mission is the measure upon which the individuals flourish or parish.

Sadly, CorporateLand is changing for the worse since the inception of feminism and SJWs alike. The model is changing from the stable and successful masculine-model to the disorganized, unproductive (less profitable) Crab Basket model that women use for social organization. We will of course address this failure and eventual demise of CorporateLand as we know it from the past at the very end of this training. Your eventual escape from CorporateLand, in brief, should be your mission and ultimate goal. Your mission is not that of suicidal, but of a Shock & Awe campaign of sorts. Your goal is to get in and get out—alive of course—or with little baggage and PTSD.

PROTOCOL| Eleven

Fishing off *the* Company Pier (Part 1)

DIPPING YOUR PEN in the company ink has been and always will be the worst thing a man could ever do at the office. There is a reason why we have these sayings and sound the alarm bells over this issue. There is a rationale for why you hear so many horror stories and few success stories when intimacy of any kind takes place between male and female co-workers—especially between males who are in higher positions than the female. However, with that said, you can employ 'catch and release' Game (window dressing) to enhance your position with females in CorporateLand. The question you are probably thinking is, *"Can I, and should I, use the Game techniques I've learned in mating strategy to forward my career in what is now becoming a more female dominated world?"*

The short answer is "yes" (especially in more female dominated industries) and the long answer will be addressed in two parts. This is part 1.

In female dominated sectors there will only be a smattering of males in and around the office and work area. You may be thinking *"So, practicing Game in female-dominated industries is probably a bad idea then, right...since a sexual harassment law suit is waiting to happen?"* Yes and no. If you try to fuck them, yes. If you Game these women in hopes of achieving EndGame then you may be looking forward to an endless horizon of diversity-training classes. The way you need to think about CorporateLand is the reality for most that are in it is merely a place for White Knights and manginas to overdose on Bluepills until they all hit menopause. In fact, a female-heavy environment such as a female-dominated workplace is often an outstanding opportunity to practice Game...with a few caveats of course. The first one is going to be confusing, too.

You Don't Practice Game at work with Intent to Seduce Anyone

Allow me to explain, gentlemen. As we already covered, women who associate together form what is called the Female Social Matrix, regardless of what the context of that association is. The Female Social Matrix (FSM) surrounds us all, everywhere, even outside of CorporateLand. Using Game at work has the powerful possibility of entangling you in a Machiavellian maelstrom of competing loyalties and petty infighting of epic proportions. Hence, GameLawRule #1 is 'Don't shit where you eat'. However, that doesn't mean you can't PRACTICE your Game here, and—this is very important— actually use some aspects of Game to *improve* your work performance and social dynamic.

The main focus of Game, after all, is ultimately to improve social dynamics, and in the service-oriented/consumer culture economy we live in, social dynamics are key to any serious professional ambitions. Therefore, using Game to improve and further your career goals isn't just *not* "unfair" it is actually in your best interest to do so. This is because despite what they say (Remember the difference between what women say and what they do) they do NOT have *your* best interests in mind. You are either there as a useful tool or an obstacle for them; and adopting any other posture in return would be career suicide.

If Game is used to counter the typical female traits of Hypergamy, Entitlement, and Solipsism (and the Shit Tests that come from all three) in dating and romance, there is no reason why you should not *also* exploit the power Game gives you to challenge and manage the females at your workplace, it's only fair. And while these suggestions won't fit every sector and every workplace in CorporateLand, you will get the gist of it. They will serve as an umbrella to use in order to shield you from the tears of all your other male co-workers; who aren't armed with the same information and in turn have lost everything; due to thinking with their peckers.

The Beta Blue Office Strategy:

The problem is most guys take a beaten-dog approach to an all-female office setting. They've become so poisoned by feminist ideology that even *they* reject their own masculinity; it colors their vision in very unhealthy ways.

For example, a fairly dominate male, who is single, and is used to hooking up three or five times a week might see the sea of cubicles, smell the estrogen in the room, and resign himself to a sort of bitter silence so as to not rouse the wrath of the HR personnel Gods.

One carless remark to the hot college intern or summer student, he's toast and he knows it. And he always seems to make that remark in front of the exact wrong person, *every* time. She might not even report it to the HR Hyenas, but she *will* talk about it with the other cackling females at the office— he knows it, too. And he knows he has trouble coming. At that point he uses the ideology of feminism as such a profound negative that he becomes jaded, and thus gains the reputation in the FSM as an angry, sexist introvert that bears watching. He reacts in turn to the consensus formed against him from the FSM and confirms their assessment by his sarcastic, bitter responses. This thus leads the Matrix marginalizing him for his "unproductive" attitude, and his work performance suffers even if his work product remains good. Since he responded callously, however, they treat him collectively like a disapproving mother, which is the go-to attitude for the FSM in that situation. What's the result for this dude then? Well, he gets passed over for a promotion since he's *not diverse enough.* He starts slinking and snaking around the edges of the office, effectively socially ostracized, his continuing displays of petulant behavior and petty feuding making him appear even less manly(ironic, I know) in the eyes about just everyone there. His co-workers are de facto opponents who just happen to have tits.

They also resent his attitude and are immediately wary of his shadow and presence in their midst. In no time at all he will soon be labelled the dreaded "Creepy" or "Angry" and either way he is not getting promoted. Does this scenario sound familiar to you? How many lads do you know who've screwed up their jobs because they went to work every morning prepared for physical battle (difference between that and mental), playing a perpetual game of quoting employee handbook regulations and puerile mocking? At that point, you can't hit anyone at work if you tried— the FSM would have formed such a strong field of consensus against you that any women who dares to break it risks losing position. Your only option is to really sit tight and hope that the company lays off half of your department due to a bad quarter. Or, pretend to be a White Knight, SJW, skinny-jean wearing prick in order to weasel and simp your way back into their good graces—taking huge losses of ManPoints in the process. Sucks to be you, if you're that dude.

The Alpha Red Strategy:

Consider once more what Game actually is at its core: a social strategy. One that is designed to ultimately get you laid early and often, however, the basis of Game is to manipulate social interactions to your advantage through using gained knowledge of human psychology, more specifically, human sexual psychology.

With that said you can apply human sexual psychology at work and have it affect your job performance without getting your penis directly involved. CorporateLand is a concrete jungle filled with females now ever since the late 1960's, so the same laws and rules apply here as they would outside of it. The very basics of Game apply to work situations just as they do in mating situations. While feminism has trained you to treat female co-workers like fellow comrades who just happen to have tits and a wet hole, and not women whose tits and tight asses you can't stop thinking about, *that's a Shit Test. If you play along you've lost.* As you attempt to suppress your feelings on the matter, grit your teeth and solider on with the burden of a hard-on and the daily emasculation on your shoulders, your attitude craps out. What you need to do at this point is back that shit up, and *re-frame.* Forget that your female co-workers *are* co-workers, for a moment, and approach them as you would the red-blooded women at the bar—by controlling the frame, first and foremost. When you set the tone and control the frame you remain in control of the interaction, which is key. Every interaction with your female co-workers should be pro-active (not reactive) and on *your* terms. When you go into those boring meetings about Mission Statements and Team Building don't just zone-out while you're waiting for the Butter-Chicken buffet to roll in—have your own private agenda in hand and pursue it respectfully, but aggressively.

When you go to see your boss about something, always have something else that you want to discuss above and beyond whatever it is she wants to discuss. Always control the frame.

By controlling the frame of every interaction, you control the conversation—making it more predictable as the outcome will not be too surprising since you'd have a general sense of where the interaction can lead to: *"I understand you're busy, but I just wanted to know if you were leaning more towards Susan or me to head up the new office?"*(Where Susan is a total, moron). Or if you've been called to account for someone else's screw-up, present the entire thing as if you're thrilled that someone is at last *"getting to the bottom of the matter"*.

If you're the only lad in an office full of women, don't slob-out like a single mom at the grocery store because you know you're not going to get laid. So why put in the effort? By taking care of your appearance and clothing, you distract women's far more weighty concerns about business. For example, a friend of mine once wore a beautiful bright yellow silk tie, hand painted, to an important presentation where he was pitching some impressive bullshit about nothing to a panel of middle-aged female execs. His female boss had him dress appropriately and even selected his tie. She wasn't an idiot—she knew how women's minds worked. Since he had on impressive shoes (bought second-hand from a show repairman), a tailored suit, and had that glorious tie on, during the meeting their eyes and attention were on his threads, not on the crap he was piling on.

Afterward, each of the female execs asked more questions about the tie and threads than they did about the presentation—and yes, he got the contract. Not because of the tie, but what the tie **represented**. It gave them something to focus on and admire, which kept them from looking at our figures and stats too closely—which were fucking atrocious by the way. A panel of dudes would have completely ignored what he was wearing, and would've called us out on our bullshit numbers.

Next, remember a fundamental truth about women: ***Never trust what a woman says, trust what she does***. That may seem to prove difficult in a workplace setting, because it's entangled in all sorts of protocols and stupid regulations. If you have a female boss, however, it is a vital thing to understand. You can try to do that latter of what she says she wants and *still* fail, in her mind though. You have to do what she actually wants, even if she doesn't know what she wants.

This implies communicating with her (or any other woman) on *two different* COMM channels: The *official* office communication channel and the *emotional* channel. When working in an office that is majority female, how they're *feeling* is as important as what they are *saying*. This is important to you, not because you need to emasculate yourself and play the Matrix games, but because knowledge is power, and knowing who is feeling bitchy that day can be as important as not getting a memo.

In fact the more you recognize the Matrix games and how to avoid them, and the more you Game the women therein the more personal power you will accrue in the office regardless of the number of women working there. That's essential.

Fishing off *the* Company Pier (Part 2)

"You can't be the dominate male at work in an office full of women, can you? Not without being the boss, right?"

Actually, you *can*.

Remember, you aren't really trying to seduce any of them; buttering their muffin accidentally is just dressing on the side. You're just trying to inspire a calculated social response to your displays, that's it. You're playing War Games, a simulation exercise. You're practicing with blunt weapons, so to speak. You don't actually want to penetrate and crush any of their pussies with your warhead; you just want the alarms to sound in and around her mountain-top facilities and bunker down below; without actually sending a payload. Since there is no real "outcome" to anticipate, you can take a few risks you might not when the possibility, or rather, pussibility is on the line. That takes an enormous amount of pressure off your Game. It doesn't have to succeed to that level or outcome.

After you've gone over your wardrobe and personal presentation, including your stance and stride, pay more attention to your verbal cues.

These become more important in an office setting than in a relationship, since (theoretically, at least) you're communicating more data signal with less emotional static there. Your word choice, tone, and inflection convey a host of information about you, and being careless with them leaves you vulnerable to the devilish nature of the office Matrix. Start by the simple expedient of insisting on 'W' words. All too often women ask us "Can you____?" or "Could you____?" instead of "Would you____?" or "Will you____?". The difference is subtle and some people would even say incidental, but I think it's important. The use of C words is a passive verbal challenge to the competency of the person in question.

The 'C' worlds imply that the person's ability to do the task in question is open to question. The 'W' words assume that you do, indeed, have the capacity to do the task, and is a simple request for you to do so. 'W' words invoke your aide; they do not challenge your competency. Why is it an important distinction? When people subtly doubt your abilities, it detracts from your Alpha presentation. When your co-workers or boss subtly beseech you for your abilities and assistance, it adds to your Alpha presentation because it is a sign of respect.

Indeed, many people—more specifically feminist-minded female supervisors—may not see this as an important distinction, out loud. However, a little social prodding can go a long way. When a co-worker asks you to do something with a 'C' word, re-direct.

"Can you take this up to HR for me?"

"I can...and I will, if you throw in a please!"

Say it cheerfully for the first time, just this side of dickish. Slightly increase the dick-headedness you use each time you are forced to do this. Don't cross any verbal lines and don't lose your composure—let *them* lose control.

Alternates:

"Can you get that to me by Friday?"

"I WILL get it to you by Friday. Why must you doubt me?"

"Can you finish that by the end of the day?"

"I can...it's a matter of whether or not I will."

"Can I get you to take that box of manila envelopes up to the third floor storage?"

"That's an interesting question—I suppose it depends on what approach you take."

You can probably glean from all of that how you skirt the edge of trouble. That's all fine, just as long as you stay clear of any serious infringements like sexual innuendos.

For example:

"Can you finish that off by the end of the day?"
"I will usually be able to do it in five at home, when there is no pressure." **winks and directs attention to one's own bulge.

Don't do this shit. You aren't out with your buddies for a couple of brews. The goal is to insist on something minor but important, and to do so across the board. Eventually someone will notice you being a dickish lad about this and call you out on it. That's the payoff you're looking for. *Finally, not everyone you work with is a full-fledged retard.* When you finally get to explain to them that you find the use of the 'C' words, in requests for your compliance, are innately condescending and you'd prefer to be asked outright with dignity. Surely, that is not too great of thing to ask of your co-workers? If you've worked in CorporateLand for a while, at some point one or more of your female colleagues will try to get you to do their work for them; they're women, remember.

They may even resort to flirting with you to convince you—not in a serious way, just throwing a subtle cat in your face/indicators of interest your way to incite your very interest; then asking you 'pretty pweeze' to do that spreadsheet for her while your thinking about motorboating her fresh produce display or deep-sea diving your submarine into her cavern, repeatedly; a rotor through her love tunnel. In other words, she is trying to make you her **Office Chump.**

Don't be an Office Chump; it demeans the rest of us in Corporateland.

Even though we've already covered the fact that you should never fuck around with bait at the company pier, it needs to be further addressed, that if you are still feeling hopeful, please know that she's never going to put-out for you. She'll be like one of those shit slot machines you'll find at the casino; no payout no matter how many greenbacks you put into it. She will never fuck you (it's very rare) and those 'LOLs' are just window-dressing.

When a woman tries to pawn her work off on you with light flirtation, it's an Office Shit Test and one you MUST NOT FAIL. When you become the Office Chump, not only are you diminished in her eyes, but you lose serious Manpoints from every other woman in the office, too. The proper response is to refuse, politely, while escalating the scope of your displeasure with each of her subsequent requests. After a pseudo-prostitute request like this is made, here are some potential responses you might want to take into consideration, with appropriate level of emotional content. Remember, in two-channeled female communication, the emoting that you do along with your response, is JUST AS IMPORTANT as the words you say:

" I'm afraid I can't help you with that today." Aloof.
"I have enough of my own work to do." Snide.
"Really? You expect me to do that? Isn't that your job?" Incredulous.
"And what makes you think I would do that for you under these circumstances?" Curious and slightly aggressive.

Side note: It won't matter what 'circumstances' exist or don't exist between the two of you at the time. By mentioning that there *are* 'circumstances,'—if she isn't aware of any—her solipsism will supply some. Are you secretly plotting against her? Do you have a crush on her? Did one of the other women say something about you or her? ACCK!

"Yeah? And I'd like you to grease my fat knob with those FuckLips you got on today, sugar tits!" You've been thinking about the exit door all day long and consider lawsuits to be fun.

"It sounds like you should've managed your time better." Amused.

"Sucks for you, hope all works out." Stoic.

"What's in it for me?" Opportunistic and blunt. Leer a bit, maybe, but don't escalate towards sexual.

"Perhaps if you are under-resourced, we could bring it up with your supervisor at the next production meeting." Ice cold.

You could also say nothing. Blank stare, snort of dismissal, silently return to your work. She and her outrageous request are beneath your notice, and she has irrevocably lost favor in your eyes. Think of her as you would a brat, a red headed step-child who just made a mess in the kitchen and then asked for a puppy. That is the disapproval you want to convey, and your silence will freak her out. Just whatever you do, please, DO NOT become the Office Chump. Try to keep strategic situational awareness active at all times: After all, you are a Sandbox dude on the Swing set side of town. You are essentially walking past all of these chicks who are swinging back and forth, asking for pushes or screaming at you to get out of their way.

You don't handle the situation by climbing on one of swings and trying to compete against the endless back-and-forth as one of the swingers, you're the cool kid on the block that has the ability to push (be a strategic ally) some of the women forward...and screw with anyone who messes with you and your BigWheel, by pushing them off their swing.

Your very own masculinity, something that feminists want to destroy, is what gives you leverage. Why? It's because women react to a man psychosexually, regardless of context. If you're the only or one of the few men in the office, like it or not your presence is still a factor in the Matrix. Being responsive in nature, women will be prone to respond to what you do and don't do, regardless of your intentions. If you're the young lad in an office full of old dried-up biddies, then they will possibly take a maternal attitude with you as they pre-judge you for suitability for their sexually frustrated daughters, granddaughters and nieces.

If you're in a mixed office with younger and older women, then the younger women will subconsciously seek your favor while the older ones will judge you harshly for flirting overmuch with the younger, tighter, hotter ones. However, the older ones will sometimes be quick to use you as a point of leverage to improve their own Matrix position (you get serious points for giving to the GoodMom foundation, regardless of your age).

Remember the two-channeled communication? That's where this comes in. If a dude on a team full of other dudes has a bad day, everyone just ignores it and focuses on their work, keeps it light and moves the fuck on. If a dude on a team full of females has a bad day...*everyone* reacts. When the "male" in the room is angry, upset, brooding, whimpering like a little bitch, every woman in the office is instantly alerted to it—as if some sort of WWII bunker alarm goes off, or the one from 007 GoldenEye—and flips the solipsism into overdrive. The reaction they have will depend on who they are, how old they are, and your previous history with them. But since the Matrix exists in the belief that negative emotions are a threat to consensus, women tend to respond dramatically to your display. A woman may work with you and never consider you seriously, one way or another...*until she thinks you're upset with her for some reason.* It's hilarious to watch. ***There is a very strong fear of being disliked in the heart of a woman, even disliked by people she doesn't personally like.*** Women are solipsistic enough to put themselves at the heart of every equation—*use* this.

The rationale behind this is Matrix-based. If you're upset with her, for any reason whatsoever, then she will *automatically* suspect that you will work against her through the Matrix (i.e. gossip, spreading rumors, and other typical weapons in the estrogen arsenal). And since you're a guy, and guy's are suppose to be all stoic and such, if you're emoting strongly then she knows that you are *likely* very upset.

Within the Matrix, such emotional issues are handled by smoothing them over, talking them out, and appealing to common experience of womanhood for understanding and sympathy. When a woman emotes strongly, it is a cry for support and assistance; even if she is bitching out like a kid. With guy's...not so much.

So, use that. Be direct. Don't bring up your obvious emotional state unless asked, and even then be highly reluctant to discuss it... but once the subject is broached, be direct, be brutal, and then be done with it. Don't dismiss your emotions in front of them (deny that you are angry or upset), but instead demonstrate that you are in control of them and re-direct.

For example, *"Chad, you seem to be...upset today. Is there something wrong?"*

"Nothing that I care to discuss with you. Let's get back to work, shall we?"

(She hears: Nothing I care to discuss *with you.* It says that you're going to pointedly ignore this obvious emotion because you're just that cool, cool enough in fact to even work with someone who has pissed you off.)

"Chad, is there something the matter...you seem agitated today?"

"Actually yes, there is. I overheard something dark being said about a co-worker by two other co-workers, and it made me uncomfortable and angry. But I'm trying not to dwell on it. I've got too much work to do to be distracted."

"Chad...I noticed you were upset over something?"

"I am... I don't want to talk about it."

In "womanese" this means "I *want* to talk about it!" and more than likely that's how your female colleague is going to interpret it: A request for a verbal prod so that you may talk about your *feeewings*. Only, you're a dude. You've been passively trained to "talked about your feeeewings" by the Marxist cesspools that are modern day universities, despite your natural inclinations, and she will probably tell you that *you'll feel better* if you talk about it. Women only feel better if they do, men don't. It actually feels even worse when you know you've been a pussy, or have demoted your manhood down to Pussified status. You're a dude. We DO NOT process our feelings by TALKING about them the way women do. We process our feelings by WORKING THROUGH THEM; often silently and with great introspection. This process of dealing with emotions is how the greats do it, all the great men that have come and gone before you. You use that anger; that hate, those "feelings" to motivate you.

You channel them into your work and most often than not, great things come from this method. Women get rid of this energy and expend it to others. They don't use it how men use it like fuel for a fire, a project, an invention or an idea. They just *piss* it away, like money. That's why men run things, why we create awesome shit. It's because women are too busy talking to each other about their feelings while we are silently crafting in the background. It's one of the main reasons why your boss or CEO is more than likely, a dude.

Our unwillingness to discuss our powerful feelings is not, as feminists claim, a weakness. It's a feature. Feminists claim that it is a weakness because they know how powerful our feelings are as a man, and how dangerous they can be in way of achieving success above them. So, when a woman encourages you to *talk about your feeewings,* she is not only trying to get you to reveal important emotional information about yourself, *she's seeking data she can use in the Matrix.* It will drain you of your leverage and power. You will feel exactly like you do after a woman drains your nut-sack on a Sunday morning.

If you're upset because Jessica was a Grade 'A' Cunt this morning, then she can *use* that. If she doesn't *know* the reason you're upset, she has to let her hamster wheel spin and the solipsism gears gyrate and go to work. That's not to say she'll be unsympathetic towards you—but you'll have to ask yourself if it is her sympathy that you want. Sympathy is not the reaction you're looking for. If you say that you don't want to talk about it, you need to establish that you're, in fact, *not* going to discuss it; any further incitements to do so will be met with frustrating looks and angry gestures. For example, you could be a temp at an office and get a lot of guff for *being mad.* Well, not "being mad"— but "being mad" and *not telling anyone why.* Let's say you get called into the manager's office to explain yourself.

You haven't done anything wrong and there isn't a problem with your production or work for that matter, however, it is because you're making your co-workers 'uncomfortable' with your emotions, when they don't even know the reason. You say that 'It's personal,' and that if they wanted to keep prying into your personal life then you'd call your temp manager to ask for another assignment.

For you, it's like the *Notebook* all over again: In the absence of real data, speculation will be substituted and used as if it were the real thing. With that said, perceived emotions can be of great value to you on the job. Just as being aloof and disinterested most of the time works wonders, so does being a tightly-controlled ball of rage. When a man in a group of women does that, I'm certain that there is some sort of phenomenal signal that causes women to be anxious on a biological level. Thanks to over 100,000 yrs of hazardous history on abuse, a man who is angry is a potential danger to women. He's also far more attractive to them. The toxic feminist argument against "Patriarchy" that revolves around female security usually includes some point about 'domineering fathers' (something I bet most feminists never had in their life, and desperately wanted) and a slap or two against the "sensitive male ego".

Making a gaggle of women squirm over your negative emotional state gives you some power over them. Think about it for a second. Denying them any data as to why gives you even more power. To close our verbal journey in this section, remember that an Alpha states where he's going and invites others along, he doesn't strive for consensus. Don't strive for consensus, that's what women do. Don't automatically go along with the team because it's 'safe' if you think otherwise; that's what lemmings do. More often than not you will get slaughtered going along with the herd. Be kind of a dick about it too, seriously. They'll be annoyed...but they won't be disinterested.

An Alpha doesn't over share, particularly about his emotional state. An Alpha doesn't request sympathy, nor demand verbal respect from his peers. An Alpha doesn't succumb or bow down to Shit Tests; he leaps over them and sets the frame. An Alpha isn't a Chump. An Alpha uses 'I' and 'Me' language and avoids trying to bury himself within a group. An Alpha seeks recognition for achievement; he doesn't want a trophy for participation. As you work on your Alpha presentation, slowly incorporate a few of these things into your office routine every week. It will become second nature over time. Expect some resistance though, some heat, pushback, and even some blowback, depending on how sensitive your co-workers and supervisors are.

However, that's kind of what you're looking for: Remember it's a fundamental Game truth that women *need* excitement—and nowhere do they need it more than in CorporateLand. When what Holly has for lunch (how much salad dressing she's using even though she's on a 'diet') is the pressing topic of conversation, you can imagine just how starved for excitement their brains are. By being a bit of a dickhead about a point like this, you are becoming the topic of conversation, and excitement. It's hardly driving through the wall of a Walgreen's with a Cadillac like a senior in Boca or driving through the halls with a motorcycle, but it's just the right hint of 'badass' to get some notice. If contorted directly by your supervisor or HR with a directive to stop—the worst you might have to deal with—tell them to go Deep Six themselves stubbornly state that it is not too much to ask for some respect for you and your job.

If they insist on a dominance display of pea-cockery for challenging their authority, reluctantly agree to stop correcting people, but point out that you have made the request, and your co-workers who ignore it are making a statement to you about their feelings. Then go brood at your desk and turn down the temperature in the office for a few days and let them freeze. Women hate it when a man broods, it makes them anxious.

Other ways to verbally express a dominant presentation include pausing for three heartbeats before answering a question—the faster you respond and talk the less in-control you sound. Practicing a sly, rakish smile that you can deliver no matter the words vacating your mouth and a dismissive sigh will automatically make women feel like pushy little brats being busted by Daddy. Above all else, keep things mysterious, my friend. Don't give them too much information and don't be afraid to be vague and non-specific.

By now you've probably been in the cubicle war for months, even years now, and the fascination that CorporateLand has with "casual Fridays" is no less than obsessive, almost borderline psychotic. It's another reason why we have such hit songs like Lover Boy's "Working for the Weekend" and restaurants like TGI Friday's. People will almost chop their leg off and threaten suicide for the right to dress down on Friday, to express themselves and relax while they pretend to work. What we are proposing with Formal Friday's is an act of gender-based guerilla ontology.

Formal Friday's

IF YOU'RE GOING TO WORK in one of these tense office environments where male-female interactions are fraught with the potential shout of sexism, misogyny or such, and particularly if you're a guy in the minority in your office, consider flouting the Casual Friday code of dishevelment and go the *other* direction. Dress like one of your male co-works who have a court date with the ex-wife, and show up smelling like an aggressive rose in the thorn bush. To get maximum effect, coordinate with as many other guys as you can, without letting any of the office ladies in on the secret. Be sure not to just dress formally, but to maintain a formal presentation—all fuck'n day long: Formal greetings and salutations, and a strict and absolute adherence to the rules of manners and etiquette. You'll surely charm the entire older Hen's house with this shtick—and more importantly—piss off any feminists, manginas, or SJW's who for some reason would rather be treated like dog shit.

Speak quietly and formally to them, open doors politely and otherwise embody the traditional male business ideal to the best of your ability; which is probably great. It will eat them alive.

Casual Fridays as a concept are embraced by corporate feminism as a means to escape the oppression of female formal office wear. Heels, nylons, make-up, and all the other feminine accoutrements expected of a woman dressed for a professional setting, and the additional layer of social/corporate matrix rules is, apparently, an affront to feminism and women everywhere. Casual Friday's is thus a small and, quite frankly, pathetic victory. By going light or no make-up and jeans and a T-Shirt on Friday's, corporate feminism can "strike back" at the Man who is keeping them down.

So...as a man ignore Casual Fridays, and institute a voluntary Formal Friday among the dudes at work, but *just* the dudes. On Friday morning, all the men will show up looking like a million dollars, with suits, ties, briefcases and the whole shtick. The women will walk in the door *sans* make-up, in jeans, yoga pants, sweats or other light wear, looking like bleary-eyed single-mommies rolling out of bed at noon. If you've seen what happens on Casual Friday's in a lot of places, you know just how disturbing that can be. Naturally, they will want to know what's up. Hell, they'll be dying to know as the hamster wheels will spin in their heads. *Wedding? Funeral? Court date? Are they all interviewing?!*

However, don't say anything beyond *"What's the matter with a man wanting to look his best?"* Throw in a cocky grin and a confident wiggle of your ass—like Patrick Bateman would—as you walk away. Under no circumstances should you give them a straight and honest answer. If they try to bust you on it, insist it was pure coincidence. Put nothing in email—this is a world-of-mouth operation.

There are two points to this exercise. The first is fairly straightforward. By assuming a formal posture while they assume a casual one, you have effectively taken the socially dominant presentation, regardless of your actual position relative to a particular woman. The division director might be four levels over you, but just watch the change in her demeanor as she slouches into the break room in a stained sweatshirt from her college days and stonewashed jeans and has to ask four smart-looking IT guys to do something for her.

This has two effects: The first being an active resentment by those women who desperately cling to the promise of Casual Fridays as the ONE DAY of the week they can relax and take off their feminine corporate Kevlar vests and armor...and you just bitch-slapped that out of their hands like bad caviar. When the VP goes around handing out paycheques or whatever, and he sees a posse of swagger in suits and power ties amid a festering wound of a cube farm consisting of ponytail scrunches and unshaven legs; it's going to get noticed, even if no one says a goddamn word about the elephant in the room.

The second effect is going to be a little more under the radar. By changing the presentation of the core male group from low Beta to high Alpha in appearance, you have collectively tossed your masculinity out on the table for the positive inspection of every woman in the joint. Women *like* guys in suits, it's a timeless fact. It's as timeless as the buzz-cut and the White T-shirt. This is thanks to a host of cultural factors involving the demonstration of value and status.

Real men (not to be confused with manginas) actually *like* suits because the basic corporate uniform is both simple and almost universally flattering. Get a shave, haircut and slap a suit on any bloke and his personal stock price goes up half a point, minimum. Coats and ties can convert a keg belly into a "stout" or "sturdy". Bald heads look better overtop a $500 suit. Gray hair? Salt and pepperboy? No fuck'n problem, because suits and gray hair were *designed* to go together.

Ties? Consider what they're pointing towards. You put a bunch of lads in suits, acting all formal, around a bunch of women in sweats and yoga pants, and there's going to be a reaction. First, the reaction of the guy's: Men just feel more powerful and more important when they are in their suits. It's the same when a man puts on a pair of Aviators; you just feel compelled to act like a total raging, dickhead. A man in a suit around people, who are dressed closely to the manner of homeless, or cat-whisperer, feels socially superior, which gives him more confidence and self-assuredness. A whole group of men feeling this way, and it's likely to get a little...*cocky* in the office.

Then, watch the Female Social Matrix at work in reaction to the unexpected suits: Make-up gets hastily applied like a clown late for a children's charity, hairstyles are quickly and quietly shifted, and body language alters noticeably, even if the complaints about the men in suits on maimed Casual Friday get loud. No matter how die-hard the corporate feminist, put her in a group around a bunch of dapper dudes and catty-mouthed women and the FSM kicks in, *hard*. Suddenly it's not TPS reports you're working on, or some other made-up bullshit, it's Prom all over again; and *everyone wants to be the popular girl*.

The other point to the operation is more subtle: It is the visible defense of the masculine business model, the one that effectively *built* CorporateLand before it became a giant VA-GIN-A in men's clothing—not to mention a business model that built a post-industrial society that allowed for such luxuries like feminism, ironically. Women "invaded" the workforce and CorporateLand in large numbers in the 1970's—before that, business was almost exclusively a man's world. While First and Second Wave feminists were trying to shoulder and "lean into" the business world, they had to compete with men (which they hate doing because it's too hard), and the female version of the male business suit—pantyhose, skirt suit, make-up and heels, the very thing that modern corporate feminists hate—became the popular and acceptable camouflage pattern and cognate to the professional suit and tie.

Then of course, the Third Wave ~~cunts~~ feminists came waddling along—causing massive earthquakes—shaking up the culture. Suddenly, those suits were now *tangible signs of an oppressive Patriarchy*, attempting to bind women's feet and keep them in their place by "requiring" an additional hour or so in preparation time that their stupid male co-workers didn't have to go through every morning; just to please the sexual sensitivities of the men in CorporateLand. Hence, Casual Friday's was born.

In establishing a Formal Friday, you are effectively challenging that idea: That corporate professional dress is inherently oppressive and any reasonable person in their right mind (and just about every feminist identifies herself as such) would want to flee the shackles of formality to focus on Getting Stuff Done. Your lads and your wall of suits is a sign of sub-textual mutiny, reclamation of the business suit as a point of masculine superiority, *not* a means of subjugation. It's you and your lads saying *"Yeah, we're men, and we're working...what are you doing?"* to the women in the office. It's a tactic designed to be collectively passive-aggressive toward the wall of estrogen in your office, a way of psyching them out by *visibly* out-performing them. Women are heavily appearance-based and shallow; that includes even men's appearances. As much as guys love to watch boobs with our ninja-like peripheral vision, women can determine a man's situation in life by a glance at his shoes.

Being in the presence of a formal presentation cannot help but make them squirm into a gooey mess. It will also make them nervous and it will make them uncomfortable on the day they revere as the most comfy of days. And the fact that none of your lads are willing to tell them why, gives you bonus Manpoints.

If even just five or six guys have a Formal Friday of their own *but don't explain themselves to the rest,* then more than likely female solipsism will seep in, to helpfully fill that void. Nervous, anxious women who don't know what the fuck is going on around them will strive magnificently to try and find *any* explanation that fits (most are likely to be absurd). And of course, they will all find a way to make *themselves* the reason. So if you do try Formal Fridays in this manner, by afternoon everyone should shut-up and pay attention to how the woman folk react; what they say and how they will try to find a way to rationalize your behavior in a way that puts themselves as the center of attention. It's hilarious!

Lastly, it is only fitting that a bunch of well-dressed, hard working guys break off after work and go have a few drinks together en masse. Once you've conquered your day, impressed the ladies, pissed off some co-workers, and generally spent your day doing nothing but look more like a CEO than a LOL, there's nothing better than to stew in the masculinity implicit in a bar. Work this right and you can all end up looking like an expensive Whiskey commercial. It might even segue into some post-work sarging at the bar; end it with a 'bang'.

Of course, with the laws of the universe, there will be an equal and opposite reaction to your shenanigans at the office. They might be subtle, at first, but any time a group of men appears to be keeping a secret together, that fact burrows under the skin of the Female Social Matrix and get's infected within days; the smell of almonds will travel fast throughout the office. You might just get a lot more attention from some of the ladies in the office—those who admire you, wet from you, and those who are pissed-the-fuck-off that you and your posse are ruining Casual Fridays. When they find out all the dudes are congregating and conspiring behind closed doors in smoke-filled merriment—over Cognac without a female co-worker in sight— well, that's just one step away from a sexist, exclusively-male Gentlemen's Club, the bane of feminisms existence.

Keep Formal Fridays up as a regular thing for a few weeks, and watch the women start to squirm. It's beautiful psychological warfare and let's face the facts, we all like to look good; unless you're some socialist, homeless hipster, who doesn't mind the stench of his own poverty and loser status.

PROTOCOL| Thirteen

Power *&* Position

WHEN PRESENTING AN ALPHA presentation in the office you need to become dominant and dynamic. The two go well together like Bailey's & coffee. There is certain body language that one uses during Single Game, Married Game, and also Office Game. In any Game situation, you want to be the dominant figure, every time. That is most important; you don't ever want to be seen as the dude on the sidelines warming the bench or stuck in the trenches or foxhole waiting for a chance at action. You want to be the Alpha. When you are attempting to assert your Alpha Presentation in the cubicle farm, paying close attention to your attire and social distance is important. Ignoring key elements of position and body language can make your spiffy PowerPoint presentation and new shiny tie look like shit. When you are competing in an office type situation (you are, even if you don't know it yet) with a number of women, then your physical presentation skills make all the difference.

There are some important points to keep in mind when wrestling with your body language: You want to be powerful or at least demonstrate **dominance**. However, you also want to be perceived as **dynamic**.

When you, my esteemed cadet, enter a room, you must do so with unquestionable Alpha-like authority. You also, however, want to be as dynamic and charming and inviting to your co-workers as possible. Dominant authority without dynamic charm is just simply boorish. Dynamic charm without the dominant aspect of authority is sycophantic; neither one of these represent a path to social and professional success. When dealing in the modern corporate environment in which your female co-workers are clearly your valued colleagues as well as competitors, there are elements of this kinesthic approach that grant you natural social advantages just by being a man; so make good use of them. Taking up maximum space, for instance, physically dominating the sphere in and around you is a great way to show your machismo. This is usually easier for us than women because we are generally larger and taller. When making gestures, do so in a broad way; so that your movements invade your own personal bubble—that's a dominant move. Key hormones are released (testosterone and Cortisol) when people hold expansive gestures and open postures for two minutes.

On the other hand, people who hold tight, conservative, closely-bond postures will have their cortisol levels measure higher in their body. Cortisol is a 'stress' hormone and thus beta-posturing, instead of Alpha posturing, will release more nasty cortisol into your system.

Don't just Talk the Talk, Walk like you Mean it

When walking, for instance, doing so with the conjecture that *people will get out of your way* is recommended—you're important, you've got important things to do and people should naturally recognize this, always. Once you start doing this people will begin to notice and soon it will be second nature, for you and for them to recognize this fact. People are natural adapters to the environment around them. So change that environment to suit your needs by setting the tone and frame that every needs to get out of your way and not the other way around.

As a man, this is a huge advantage. For one thing, men don't wear silly heels, constraining skirts or nylons which allow our stride to be longer and more decisive. When a woman strides that way, she takes the risk of looking masculine and will evaporate whatever potential advantage her confident strike might give her by elevating her true value as a woman: Beauty and femininity. When a woman expects people to get out of her way it naturally comes off as entitled, pushy, cunty and not authoritative; just annoying. It is a double-standard, but it is the same way in which a man comes off as weak or pussified when he lets people treat him like a doormat: It's not attractive on a biological level. That is why SJW's have no place in CorporateLand or in any other reality.

A simple way to undermine a female competitor's position is to point out her gait or pushiness to her female co-workers (her male co-workers don't care, believe me) or inferiors. The fact that such an observation has been made by you, a *mere male*, will confirm the catty suspicions in your female co-workers minds, and before the end of the day everyone will remember her as " that pushy woman"—and 'pushy' is no authoritative. It's uncouth.

Get with the Team, the Correct Way

When you join a pre-established group of colleagues—who have already established their own inside jokes, camaraderie and workplace culture— get the lay of the land within the first couple days, but soon start executing your style therein after. The honeymoon phase for the 'new guy' will run out faster if you don't pull the cord soon enough and you will drop like a rock. Now, if you're looking to go into CorporateLand without wanting to be in the limelight or shake things up then it's ok to be a recluse and just fuck the company for the paycheque until you leave 6 months to a year later.

However, for the LongGame, you have to play the Game sooner rather than later. Don't hover anxiously like a horny schoolboy around the fringes of the dance hall if you want to participate. If you want to participate, then gently shoulder your way in or say something witty or charming that convinces the group to part and naturally invite you in. Glide in effortlessly, like you would into that hot new intern, in your wildest fantasies. When speaking to a group, keep your head perfectly still while you talk. Excess movement's make you look like it's the 1980's and you just did coke in the bathroom—indecisive and flighty. Remaining still is another advantage to Team Male in consideration of how many women feel compelled to tilt their heads around like pigeons to see if anyone is paying attention to them.

Speak slowly, deliberately, and of course in complete fucking sentences. It makes you seem thoughtful and engaging, while female co-workers have a habit of interrupting themselves, using inappropriate slang (or even baby talk), and getting off topic very easily. Don't attempt to look smart by using long winded sentences—Alphas tend to use short, concise, complete sentences with a clear beginning, middle, and end— they also don't explain themselves unless asked to. This lends an air of personal authority that no mere title can provide.

On the subject of to that, when you are speaking to someone, maintaining a nearly threatening level of direct eye-contact increases your importance in their mind. When you act disinterested with wavering eye-contact that makes you look distracted and shows you have more important things like to: Look around, scratch that itch, stare at that chicks rack and ass. You know you wanna. Further, you *don't* want to react to what your competitors have said—acting bored and distracted says more. If you allow your reactions to her to be perceived, then her importance to you is also established by the casual observer. Ignoring her or patiently enduring her while she speaks established dominance over her. Interrupting to make an important point or to ask a question are ways of establishing dominance over a competitor.

Take half a step forward when you do this, as physical movement attracts attention. However, don't anxiously scan everyone's face for signs of approval after you've spoken. *Alphas don't give-a-shit what other people think* because they themselves are the chosen ones. So, obviously checking for reactions is *not* Alpha.

Taking a dominant position in an office or a meeting is a risk— Alpha's take risks, and men generally excel at doing so. It's a sign of high testosterone and a heavy natural leader. Women are far less likely to take risks, which often keep their professional ambitions in check arterially—they are their own worst enemy. Floating a few trial ideas you *know* won't work, but are risky and demonstrably creative, for example, is a great way to establish your ability to take risks and establish your authority.

There is a danger of course with doing this. The risk is that when you present Alpha in CorporateLand, you run the risk of attracting social ire from those who feel you are inflating your status above its actual origin. For example, only the CEO can get away with *acting* like a CEO. When you try to punch above your perceived position and rank you're really acting like a douchebag. However, this risk is a lot less for men than it is for women.

When a man makes an ambitious, risky move in his career, one that could conceivably elevate his status accordingly, then the irrationally overconfident demeanor is seen as daring and confident by outsiders on the bench warming up for their turn out of the dugout. The same emotions expressed by a female competitor are usually seen as her "getting big for her britches", followed by sadly shaken hands.

Sure, it's not fair— but *it's a competition*, a Game, remember? You're always, not matter how much you hate this idea, playing a giant fuck'n game in CorporateLand: A game of either who will retire sooner, or who will survive next quarter earnings; when the layoffs start coming down from the top brass. Tit's, ass and snatch are unfair too, but we have to contend with those. Women in general are promoted for their achievements. Men are promoted, in general, for their potential. Recognizing (casually) that your female competitor may have bitten off more than she can swallow to the right set of ears is an ideal way of undermining everyone's perceptions of her. "Big for her britches" infers that she does, indeed, have limits to her capability; while you *do not*. That will also set the stage for her first few (inevitable) stumbles, and magnify and put doubt into everyone's confidence in her ability.

For the dudes, being underestimated is usually a good thing—we're competitors. We actually *want* to be underestimated because the element of surprise is key to winning a battle and a fight against the enemy. Look at the recent Trump victory against the Clinton campaign during the 2016 U.S Presidential election— that is the best example to date of how hubris and an underestimation of one's opponent can lead to a landslide victory of *epic* proportions. Sun Tzu was laughing in his grave the moment Trump won, *at* Hillary. For women, however, being underestimated means that they are also *under-appreciated,* that they aren't getting enough attention, so they loath it. When someone expresses doubt in a dude's progress, it often makes him double-down on his efforts and look forward to his day of vindication and the ultimate humiliation of his doubters and haters.

When someone expresses doubt in a woman's progress, it doesn't take long through the Matrix to get back at her...and the result can be devastating. Women seem far more likely to let others' perceptions color the choices they make and ultimately adhere to the boundaries people set *for* them.

Your Face is the 'Tell'

Most important point, don't smile too much. So many management books, seminars, and "gurus" drill the importance of smiling in your work interactions, but *don't*, unless you have a *genuine* reason.

Smiling all the time is not genuine because nobody is that fucking happy 24/7; unless you do lines of coke in the bathroom all day long or just won the lottery, in which case you wouldn't be working in CorporateLand. Beta's and women smile because they are submissive. Alphas smile because they are, rarely amused. When you speak, speak calmly and in short sentences, but smiling usually means you DON'T KNOW WHAT THE FUCK IS GOIN ON since this is business and business is serious. A smile is a sign of appeasement, not amusement. Those who do this in CorporateLand represent the visual ass-kissing of the Alpha or boss. Just like in regular Game, in Office Game eye-contact is key. If your boss is speaking, listen thoughtfully, especially if other people are watching. When it comes time for questions, ask one that you know your boss knows the answer to, and hold eye-contact when doing so...then look away.

If you lock eyes with a female competitor, DO NOT drop your gaze. Most women are more intimidated by being stared-down than they're willing to admit, and when it happens unexpectedly it can be unnerving. If she persists, slowly shift your gaze about an inch below her eye...it makes you look more intimidating for no reason she can consciously see.

When going Beta can be Alpha

You're probably wondering *"So when do you play dominant?"* Not all the time—Remember, you're not the CEO. The two areas in which you want to focus your dominant presentation are: When you need to strongly re-enforce your own status in the group and when there is a power or position available that you covet. If someone challenges your ability to do your job, you go dominant on that muthafucker to re-establish your place. If there is a higher position available, then making a dominant presentation is the easiest way to secure it over the vultures. When is it a dominant move then to play submissive? This is a lesson that most women won't understand and that most men will naturally be able to pick up on. Most women botch this lesson over and over because of this lack of understanding. So, the "Fun Fearless Female" of Cosmo fable often *loses* status and position because of their ovaries-to-the-wall attitude and inability to demonstrate the *appropriate* level of submission to a superior. I once watched a woman talk her boss out of promoting her by assuming too familiar an attitude—being "just girls" doesn't work well in a corporate setting. And when this same female treated a senior male like an equal, even to the point of correcting him about something unimportant—the consequences were staggering. Also, telling your boss to go "fuck himself" thinking that you're "equal" and entitled to because of "Rah Rah GurlPower" and the "Fun Fearless Female" mentality won't end well for the little ladies, either.

Nobody in CorporateLand will put up with that shit; this isn't a university or college feminist 'safe space'. You will get <u>crushed</u> by *reality* here.

When speaking to or presenting to a superior, appropriate. With men, treating them with respect and deference from a position of strength gains you respect and admiration in return. Telling them to go *"fuck themselves"* may seem like you're fearless, but ultimately, you're just a moron. With women, cordial and charming work best, however, cordial and charming from a strong but submissive position. When speaking with a male superior, you should leave him with the feeling that he has a potential follower. When speaking with a female superior, you should leave her feeling that she has a potential ally...against the other women under her command.

If done properly, you make your submission into a dominant act by enriching and ennobling your superior with your respect, deference, charm and strength. Done stupidly and you look like a fawning asshole. Many women seem to have a really, *really* hard time with this—either due to the fact that they are unable to distinguish themselves appropriately to demonstrate their strength to their superior, or because they shy away from self-promotion.

The fact that men and women are perceived differently in the business world is pretty well understood and will never change. Both genders have to recognize their strengths and work on their weakness in order to be successful. It just seems that men are more likely and willing to do this for reasons we've just outlined. Women don't need CorporateLand as much as men. In our society there seems to be multiple safety nets for women to fall back on: The government, other men and marriage to a man who works in CorporateLand. If you are going to go work for CorporateLand, go in alone—and come out alone and alive. Most men go in alone, then marry and have kids, get divorced and are thus stuck in CorporateLand for eternity. Don't be that guy. Get in and get out. Complete your mission, and then retire to some bay by the ocean.

PROTOCOL| Fourteen

Women *of* CorporateLand

WORKING WITH WOMEN in the modern corporate landscape, it's not as fun as it used to be; for both men and women respectively I might add, mostly because of the SJW thundercunts who've ruined equilibrium. Notice how I didn't say 'equality' but 'equilibrium' as there is a *very* big difference between the two. In fact, there was more in the way of equality between men and women when things were in equilibrium between the sexes. Everyone knew their role, and the machine that is CorporateLand chugged along smoothly. Today, CorporateLand is on its last sprocket and the oil and coal to burn is running out, thanks to SJW corporate policies and ridiculous regulatory directives that do nothing but create an environment of backstabbing, laziness, entitlement, and above all else: unproductiveness.

Most of the reasons why Corporateland is on the decline are because of the new type of woman that is entering the workplace: The Thundercunt.

There are two types of women in the office: Pre-Wall (Under age 28) and Post-Wall (over 30).

For the Post-Wall/Mother Hen types

Utilize "classic" Western chivalry. Hold doors, offer help if they are carrying something heavy, etc. Why? It's because *they* will actually respect this, the younger women won't. The older women have become—or are in the process of becoming—obsolete and unused to attention from men. You aren't Gaming them, at all, but just trying to be helpful and nice; like a normal fucking person. The younger women won't see it like that though. Being a normal person is 'Creepy' and holding doors open makes them believe that you have something up your sleeve: Modern women are mentally ill. You can be Blue Pill with these older types, like mama taught you. It's OK, you're not trying to bang them anyways and you will score huge points with the older crowd for this. An example of being considerate with the Mother Hens would be if you like to work in the early evenings or come in later at night to get a head start on a project.

Nobody is around to pester you, so you can get three solid hours of work in instead of the two you normally get out of an eight hour work day. Make a point to drop by the desks of any woman, if they are around (the Mother Hen types love this) and exchange pleasantries. Women working alone at night can be a bit jumpy, so doing this as soon as you come in won't scare the shit out of her if she suddenly bumps into you accidentally later when she thinks nobody is around.

For the Pre-Wall/Baby Chicks

You want to run *light* Game, but never give the impression that it's anything more than 'in fun'; because HR doesn't have much of a sense of humor. Keep it light and fun, stylish, not overt; and for God, Fuck'n Sakes, no goddamn KINO (touching). A lot depends on who you are and what your style is. We've all had the boss who is a total perv towards women in the office, but he gets away with it of course since he is the white-haired silver-fox, grandpa type. You can always see women doing the math in their heads and he always seems to fall above the age line (i.e. a younger guy would have gotten nailed for it). Late 40's you can easily camouflage yourself as the "Kindly Uncle" (as opposed to 'Creepy Uncle'; it's important) when need be.

There are of course the exceptions. If the chick is a SJW or otherwise, psycho, maintain a perimeter and keep interactions at an utmost minimum; only 'hello' and 'goodbye' are good. These chicks are landmines and anything you do or say will be held accountable in a court of Fucked In the Head.

A final point about the young hotties: The young, tight types—even the marginal ones are going to have what is called "Young Hot Chick Privilege" rocking 24/7. They're used to it and they don't want to give it up, even though they are at WORK. Too many young women in CorporateLand spend their life's time being Too Cool for the Universe, only to arrive at a stall in their 30's; wondering, like a kid whose spilt spaghetti all over the kitchen floor, where is Daddy?

Here are some Samples:

You work with an older lady, in her 50's let's say, who you can tell was a smoking hot babe back in the day before Elton John even knew he was gay; and who many guy's in CorporateLand would've happily banged. Even one of the gay guys would've banged her, that's how hot she was. Anyway, let's say you and her now have a very friendly relationship as you're both natural extroverts, and you're good at greasing her deals through the corporate chain of command.

A lot of younger women in the office will look up to her as a role model of sorts, thus, she provides you with a ton of social proof as she is naturally flirty, touch feely with you in social (like after hours) situations.

Similarly, let's say you work with a woman named "Sherry", who is well-past the Wall, has four kids and has never lost the baby weight and has packed on a bunch more besides that fact— and likely hasn't had her muff dusted for cob-webs by a Man broom or has been railed by her husband since the first Clinton Administration. So as it turns out, you're a singer (just go with it) and she just so happens to walk into the coffee room one day while you are pouring a cup while singing a few bars from Steve Perry's "Oh, Sherry". Now, clearly you're just being amusing, but it does make her day.

Do you do this from a sociopathic, Machiavellian perspective? Not really. You are happy to make Sherry smile and you enjoy the hot sales chick's company, in addition to the social proof she provides you. Life is short and work sucks, huge royal balls. Why not have fun? And if the fun pays out dividends, it's even better.

When you're the FNG (Fuck'n New Guy)

When you're the Fuck'n New Guy, keep your goddamn mouth shut, ok? Only until you learn the terrain first. These things will be revealed over time. Some people leave obvious clues in the cubes/offices, others do not. Listen more than you speak and proceed from there. Find out who is reliable and who isn't. Avoid having a female boss if possible, but they seem to be everywhere nowadays for no good reason other than someone propping them up, blackmail, favor, or they know someone's Daddy— or are someone's daughter. If not, an older one who 'gets it' is ok. There once was a very senior lady boss who I went to war with 7 out of 7 days of the week. Why? It was because she totally thought like a dude. I was convinced she couldn't wear miniskirts because then everyone could see how hairy her balls were.

The real problem is communication style. Women tend to be more obtuse and say things like *"Oh, whenever you get it"*, when they really mean *"By noon, tomorrow"*. You shouldn't have to do this, because you'd think you were dealing with a grown adult and not a child, but with a female boss, try to emphasize clarity if she does this shit. Ask (I know, you shouldn't have to) for specific milestones/deadlines/etc., and things will go more smoothly. Women make horrible bosses and managers for this reason alone.

Oh, and it's not just us men. You know who else prefers having a male boss? Women do. More than we do actually, by a lot. Why? It's because women *understand* other women and their games, and they hate each other. Male bosses are more predictable, mood-wise etc.

Regarding direct reports, women are going to have more problems/drama/ come in later, leave earlier and take more sick days. Those are just the facts and are pretty common sense. It's part of the reason why men EARN more. From a hiring standpoint, if CorporateLand is to survive, it should hire mainly the ugly and skilled over young & big fuck'n tits; even if she has talent. Young & Big Fuck'n Tits, even if she has talent, will still have DRAMA. You will end up doing, or delegating, Y&BFT's work eventually.

Women of Corporateland

The Lazy Office Ho'

We've all come into contact with one of these gems or you will be eventually if you're a GreenHorn to CorporateLand. She is a total pain in the ass. She has her boss wrapped around her finger and is a lazy fuck. Always agitating for more money—she knows that the last woman who had her job before her got paid way more; of course that woman had a shit-ton more talent most likely. This chick will most likely sport the 'Rocker Chick Slut Look,' have a nice body, yet have a butter-face or some other defect to go along with her sub-par work ethic and personality.

When you see this woman you will most likely think to yourself *"Gee, that vag has probably seen more sausage than a German butcher."*

She will complain a lot around the office and you will finally want to tell her that if she'd *put more effort into doing work as she did trying to get out of it, she wouldn't have any problems.* When this chick is hired it is usually the call of the HMFIC (Head Military Figure in Charge), don't go easy on her. The Hen's always think you will go easy on this chick, because she looks like she could suck a bowling ball through a chain linked fence. However, if you don't go easy on her, the Hens will love you for it; because women *hate* other women, especially the hot ones—also if she is a Lazy Ho'. When the Lazy Ho' tries to make a move on you with the Department Chair, the Hens should have your back and lock in and around you like a Phalanx. The rebellion should be crushed, mercilessly— that's another reason to cultivate and butter-up the Hens.

You're going to find a lot of good women and people in CorporateLand, though. You just have to vet and understand who you are dealing with. If you think someone is a bit sketchy, leave the door to your office open or have a 3rd party present in the meeting, if possible. Or, meet in the conference room.

The Nosey Nancy

Once upon a time there was this girl in a department who was an intern. She was always moseying her way into conversations that didn't involve her. So, many in the office took to closing their doors when they had the other intern—who was a chill and cool guy— so they could talk about sports, politics and pussy without "Little Sister" eavesdropping on everything.

For some reason this then constituted as "intentionally excluding her". Or so the chick from HR said. Now, when she asked if anyone was intentionally excluding her most of the guys responded with something akin to, *"If you mean I'm excluding you from conversations that are none of your business but that you want to hear because you are nosey, than, yes!"*

So all the king's horses and all the kings' men around the office began to give this little shit some work to do (hush and shut-up work). And when she was done, they gave her more... and more..and more work. Maybe she even did some, but the men didn't care; because it was nonsense, but it made her *feel* important and kept her out of their way.

The end.

The Always 'Sick' Girl

Women take more sick days. They come into the office later and they leave early. When they eventually have kids (most do), they get sicker, since evidently, there are institutions called "schools" or "pre-school" in which disease stricken kids play with each other in close quarters due to the prison like nature of the education system. The mommies bring that shit into CorporateLand and then infect everyone like the movie *Contagion*.

Oh yeah, and when they are out sick or taking maternity leave, they will (or your boss will) expect you to cover for them, for free! Yes, you don't get extra pay or any compensation; even though they all get a paid vacation of 12 months, sitting on their ass watching Dr. Oz all day while they manipulate their husbands to do all the baby-work. You're a male and this society shits on males; so don't ever expect the favor to be returned because of Briffault's Law and because there will be some sort of dance recital, cheerleading practice or cub scout meeting that gets in the way. This is probably the number one most frustrating reason why men are leaving CorporatLand in droves; and maybe why you should reconsider joining the ranks. However, we shall continue with the training. Onward.

The Chick Who Can't Do her Job

Everyone hates this girl, and if you're not hot, even more so; because if you're hot it is at least one thing you are good at. People leave their jobs over these types, I'm being serious. If there was an actual statistic out there to show what percentage of people leave their jobs due to this kinda Chick, I would say at least 60%, if not higher. I knew a guy in the biz that left his job over one of these.

It was time for him to move on to bigger and better things in CorporateLand, but this chick could *not*. Do. Her. Fuck'n. Job. She knew that my friend could, though. In fact, the extra work would have been easy for him to do, and would have only marginally added to his workload. This gal also had this fucked up idea that she could *order* my friend to do it, and when that failed, she resorted to *screaming*. She acted like he was Mr. Rumplestiltskin and he was suppose to stay up late and spin straw into gold for this snatch...for free—The gull, really. Big cunt, I tell ya. So, this guy bailed and found a new job with fewer issues and a substantial salary boost. It pays more to leave a job than to hope or go for a raise like we've covered already. When my friend left the old gig, he turned back a project this chick had managed to get her boss to assign him (which he, in fact, could do), with a note on it that said to the effect that he was leaving the company, and *wasn't* going to get to it before he left.

This project involved approximately <u>six thousand pages</u> of review and he made sure to hold on to it, and then return it on the Friday before the holiday weekend. When someone *tries* to fuck you, or fuck with you, make sure *you actually* fuck them in the end. A harsh lesson is the best one. This guy is forever my hero and he is still well known around CorporateLand for his vengeance.

Ms. Selfish

Women will often want something because someone else has it. Any time I hint, even remotely, that I am taking a week's vacation or two, I've had one co-worker consistently chime in that she too "might" take some days that week; even if she had just gotten back from a vacation. It's a bizarre thing to witness. I'm not averse to changing it up, with enough notice (i.e. before tickets are bought, and I try to avoid school vacation weeks that my co-worker may need. In one case, I flipped the week before Labor Day to the week after because school was starting or some shit, and one of my co-workers wanted to spend the last week of summer with her kid, that's fine. I don't have kids or any rocks in my backpack that will ultimately weigh me down, so I have a life anyways, most people around here don't. It wasn't a problem because I can literally take whatever fuck'n time off or month I'd like. The other thing is, she *asked* me. So, no biggie. However, now I just take the days and everyone else can deal; Seniority and freedom, muthafuckas!

The Ditzy Flirt

So, you know those Attention Whores you see all the time on Instagram? Yeah, well, a lot of them have jobs in CorporateLand and you might end up working with one. Whatever you do, don't fall for her *"Who, me?"* come-ons and bullshit routine. She's just looking for you to validate her massive ego and ultimately, her insecurities. It's not worth your gig, unless you're about to leave CorporateLand for good. Then I say, go fuck her in the broom closet; while Javier cleans up your mess later with a mop and bucket.

You're probably thinking in your head *"But...lots of people bang co-workers!"* I did, too. I use to have a thing, a long time ago, with an admin I worked with— who pretty much had the Rear of the Year. My loft was close and she was DTF, so we'd hop on over to it once or twice a week and have some fun, always leaving and arriving back separately. **Important Point:** If you *must* bang someone from work—for God, fuck'n sake—pick someone with more to lose than you have. My "work plate" was engaged. There was an understanding that the Fun Would End before her wedding, and it did. Now she is married and her kids (thank you Jesus) were all fathered by her ~~sucker~~ husband, who is a TOTAL Betabux. This makes sense why she wanted to fuck around with me; she knew she was getting the Golden Ticket out of life: Marriage. Which is a clean break out of Whore Island, penitentiary.

Marriage for women is a clean slate; absolving them of all past permitted dicks that motored through their cavern. What hubby don't know, hubby won't care. Poor guy though, I got the best of her. He was also worried about me, big time. She told me about it, once, after sex. So I said to her, *"What does he have to worry about? I'm only fucking you. He can have you back when I'm done"* she giggled after this. Big whore.
Even the 'Good girls' fellas...even the good girls...

This is Important

Determine the "good citizens" of CorporateLand, who can be counted on. Take care of the admins—someday you're going to need a friend in your corner. You always want to keep a positive balance in the Favor Bank.
I used to joke that, if I ever announced that I cut off my girlfriend's head (she was a plate, really, but not a distinction you should make at work) then Kayla (my admin) would appear with a hatbox of appropriate size, dispose of the evidence, and never speak of it again. You can't buy loyalty, you can only inspire it.

Debriefing

EACH AND EVERY MAN has his own reasons why joins the daily grind. Back in the 1950's the reason use to be very cut and clear and the rewards for joining the ranks use to be fruitful, just, and beneficial for the family unit. Today, it's not like this. The rewards are minimal and the reasons for joining are decreasing by the day with the every declining nuclear family model and the increasingly dysfunctional state of affairs with marriage and divorce rates. Men are being financially raped left and right for their hard work and are not being rewarded for it anymore; instead they are being taken advantage of due to the modern day mantra that is anti-male in nature. Men are now seen as disposable cogs in the new fem-centric dystopia which has produced such decay in the once great American landscape. Long gone are the managers from the World War II generation that saw corporate America rise above the skyline in new and great heights.

Now we are seeing great companies being torn down from within and are being replaced with legions of inept, scum whose only accomplishment was having economic growth, getting the largest bank bail-out in the history of the United States and sending the U.S into the largest financial crisis since the Great Depression.

Gone are the days of stable employment and all the goodness that came with it. There are no more pensions, you don't get health care, and you can bet your fucking asshole on Red you won't be getting paid your worth. You won't be getting that nice 30 years of life-long employment that once made a 30 year mortgage a relatively risk-free offer. Why fight now if not for yourself? I say, fuck the 30 year mortgage and fuck the old way of building a "life" for you. The old ways just aren't jiving with the new ways and new world we are living in. Women aren't the same and companies sure as hell aren't with all the new and useless policies that aim to destroy the hardest working employee's: Men. Companies now only reward the lazy and the victimized. On top of that, now you can get outsourced even if you're the best at what you do. You will now train your own replacements and be perpetually employed as a contractor, and let go if your job can be done for a fraction of a cent cheaper in China. Being a contractor is probably the only viable way to survive now in corporate America as a man. If you work it right you can just pump and dump while vacationing with your off-time.

A bachelor is thrilled with this prospect and corporate lifestyle because he has zero chains waiting for him in suburbia (wife & kids). The contractor life is the way to go. You adapt with whatever is being given and actually it's for the better; in regards to men in the modern era. You will be rewarded more by putting in less time while also keeping your liabilities to a minimum. Your main reward will be time.

You will have more time to do what you want instead of wasting all of your time by doing things you really don't want to do and to have people be ungrateful for your efforts.

What has spawned all of this change?

We can't forget the wave of psychotic political bullshit these past 20 years that has infected Corporate America to which chides the morality and honor of good, honest workers, particularly of the male persuasion. There is the HR lady epidemic where we put power hungry hippos who are inept, math-impaired Twenty-Something ditzes at the helm of our hiring process; who will then hire more inept people of their ilk into the fold causing the mess we see today with all the PC bullshit and social justice warrior crap. It never fucking ends now with the bullshit you have to deal with. There's "Corporate Social Responsibility" where we force unrelated and unnecessary political crusades on our employees; be it donating to the United Way, mandating weekends be spent on charities, or wearing pink every year.

There's diversity, sexual harassment, and sensitivity training where we blatantly treat all men like sexual predators, molesters, rapists and racists, humiliating them to attend said training while not holding women to any standards themselves.

There's the eggshell environment men get to work in, where a dude is one false sexual harassment accusation away from being fired. There is also the invasion of privacy into the personal lives of employees where the politically correct Corporate Gestapo will fire you over a facebook post or Tweet. There's also the rabid progressive credentialism where the HR Reichstag demands you have ten years experience and a Master's degree for entry level job's that can be done by anyone with who's a functioning adult. There's the blatant sexism against males as previously addressed before with clearly sexist policies favoring less-qualified women for the sake of filling a 'diversity' hiring quota. Top it all off with the raw deal in the number one cause of most divorces, marital strife, and problem child: commutes. If it was the 1950's-1960 and corporations were roaring along and supported by a fairer and meritocratic marginal class, I could see Corporate America being a place you would want to serve and be. Back in the day you'd be compensated for excellence, hard-work, and dedication to the force. You'd be promoted for being innovative and thinking creatively. It was a reasonably justified system which ran logical to the bullshit we have now.

It was a system of loyalty, stable employment and corporate corruption was at a minimum (at least compared to today).

Ultimately you have ask the question *who the fuck wants to work any part of the rotten deal that is corporate America?* I made myself ask that while I was newbie here and I made a promise to my soul. That promise was that I would sacrifice a small portion of it to get the thing I wanted most—money. I told myself I would make the sacrifice as painless and as short as possible, so I busted my ass in a slash & burn fashion in this world to get in and get our quickly. The catch-22 about getting what you want out of life is that you first need lots of money. To do awesome things in life, you need money. Don't listen to the hippies and the stupid hipsters with their lazy mentality that the world owes them something.

You first have to go out into world to get your pound of flesh and then you can do whatever the fuck you want after the grind. The problem though for most individuals is that you have to do it smart and try to do it as quick and efficiently as possible so that you aren't grinding until your 65 years of age and your grave is starting to call you from the echoes of the near future. I am not joking. I'm not saying all of this to disparage the workforce or that I don't want you to do what I did. It's all just a fair warning and I am not going to sugar-coat it for you like mommy would.

CorporateLand was a simulation as you've come to experience, real-world buildings but filled with fake-people. The programs we ran for you and the simulations were all taken from 'real-world' examples in order to give you an experience that could come close to the real deal.

Corporate America, you have to understand, is a horrible place for any self-respecting man (or woman) who wants to live a free, healthy, happy, sane and prosperous life. Think about it for a moment. You have to, at minimum, attend school for a quarter century, and face daunting odds of landing a job. That job now will at best entry-level and mundane. You're then forced to go out and get a Masters if you have any hope of 'making it' due to progressive credentialism. You are a mere merger away from being let go or laid off. Your compensation is significantly lower with both sexes now flooding the labour market, lowering the wage you command. You can't have a political or social life your employer doesn't approve of.

Compensation and promotion is increasingly based on your sex and skin color, not your merit or hard work. Now, if this already wasn't such a shit deal, it's all under a psychotic environment; where bosses who know they have you by the balls unleash their sadism on their employees simply to get their rocks off. There is just no godly reason now to be a part of Corporate America.

The other question though is, then, why do women seem so desperate and adamant on joining up with Corporate America? Why do they seem so obsessed over having a corporate career to the point they'll get one via legitimate means or not? The answer is they've been sold a bill of goods.

The biggest lie Ever sold...to Women

Just like the housing crisis, educational or dotcoms bubbles, women are buying into one that is about to burst. Corporate America is a dinosaur that is about to see a huge flash and firery dust cloud in the near future as our economy switches from the old industrial model to a more E-conomy where one can make his way remotely as a digital nomad through the internet. Women go to college (a bubble and increasingly poor investment unto itself) at rates higher than men, earning the majority of worthless liberal arts degrees, also now accounting for the majority of worthless masters/advanced degrees. With these worthless degrees, they then throw themselves onto the Omaha Beach of Corporate America where they forfeit family, children, husbands, a social life, and loved ones, all in exchange for promotions, careers, 2-hour commutes, and AppleBee's. They obsess about 'leaning in' and the 'glass ceiling'; getting the latest certification, credential, or promotion in their lives.

Congratulations if they even make it near those magical six figures. But to what end? The thing is, nobody gives a fuck anymore. Not only do they have to suffer the unacceptable environment laid out for them, basically ruining and sacrificing their lives, but all so they can become Queen Crab of ShitLand? Alas, it's obvious women didn't consciously decide one day on their own to pursue such a raw deal that is Corporate America. They were duped, lied to, propagandized by the psychological warfare machine that is feminism and the liberal left. They were fooled into becoming corporate slaves. Any simple, logical pondering will come up with the main culprits that misled women into choosing such a lopsided deal. First, blame the men. Seriously. Not consciously, or maliciously, but men are to blame because I don't think they ever truly conveyed to women what they endured in Corporate America when women were all shouting for the 'right to work' and 'equality'—working a real job to support the family financially. In the past, traditionally, men went to work, brought home the sack of potatoes and lard, and in order to have a peaceful and enjoyable home, they didn't bring back their work with them. They didn't talk about it or wanted to talk about it when they walked through the door and said "Honey, I'm Home!" Men, for the most part were silent at home and that's why you always saw the old stereotype about the husband who just wanted to sit in his favourite chair with a beer and watch the game. The wife didn't want to hear about the conditions of working on the railroad, the loneliness of being a travelling salesman, or the politics of a corporate office, and the man frankly didn't want to talk about it either.

He wanted to eat a good meal, lay on top of his wife— i.e. Blast a hole into her forever— play with his children, and enjoy his free time. This then misled the women into thinking somehow work was fun. And not only was that work fun, it was MUCH MORE FUN AND REWARDING than being a homemaker, housewife and mother. They only saw the financial upside of Corporate America, not the labour and responsibility that came with it. That is though women's fault into not caring about how the sausage is made; they just only seem to care about wanting that sausage and not worrying about how to get it. Then, once they realize that making sausage takes a whole lot of work, time and effort they then just walk away and get someone else to do it for them. The thing is, you can't just walk away in Corporate America when the going gets tough; unless you want to be fired or you're sucking the boss off after hours. Men don't have that luxury of blowjob insurance—types of 'workplace security' for select women.

Secondly, feminism is the other culprit to blame. The greatest scam ever pulled in the history of humans was not social security, nor buying Manhattan from the Indians for some beads. It was the con job that bitter, angry, ugly, jealous, contemptuous women from the 60's and 70's pulled by convincing their prettier, younger counterparts that being a mother or a wife was not 'real work'; hence, the Crab Basket working on a much grander scale. Think about that for a second.

It was fooling *three* full generations of women that they didn't need men, and that a paycheque (Government or Corporate America issued) couple replace a passionate kiss from a loving husband and a swarm of hugs from their children. The fact that women are trying to practically break into Corporate America by the droves, by any means possible, moral or not, sexist or not, while forfeiting a life of staying at home and spending time with their children (raising stable children instead of future carjackers) is jaw dropping once you can remove the hood of leftist, feminist brainwashing. No sane, self-respecting person would do that back in the 1950's, let alone in today's sadistic and enslaving corporate environment.

Thirdly, politicians are to blame just as much for the hoodwinking. Like feminists, it is amazing to see the con job the Democrat party pulled on women. By understanding a woman's psychology, politicians and social engineers alike made women jealous of what men had, and not appreciating what they had and how good it was compared to the hell men had to go through daily. Politicians created a problem that didn't even exist. Just like early marketing agencies in the 50's they created a *need* that was never there before and sold it to the masses as something of a void that needed to be filled in order to be a complete person.

Politicians thoroughly convinced women they were oppressed, discriminated against, and that sexism was rampant. Little did women know that they'd be the ones truly oppressed when entering Corporate America and the working world soon thereafter. Before women went to work, men were the ones truly oppressed, slaves dressed in suits and ties, chained by the Man and bound to servitude in the factories and offices for 8-12 + hours a day. You can literally go fuck yourself if you think for one second that women were ever truly oppressed before they earned the right to be a corporate slave. How fucking ironic. Women by now understand this as both men and women today can experience the joys of oppression together while working at the office together! Congratulations! Politicians would enforce affirmative action policies, Title IX, give you a never ending litany of PSA's and speeches blasting those evil males for their inherent sexism and privilege, and as an added bonus, designate the government as your sole supporter and provider making those nasty evil men unnecessary and obsolete. When all the while the very nasty and evil people (both men and women) were the politicians who were creating this; it was all designed to put women in the same chains as their men. It was designed to capture the other half of the tax pool. The propaganda was so it actually overrode women's genetic programming to the point they actually believed for a moment in human history "women need men like a fish needs a bicycle."

And if you needed more proof as to the completeness of the con job, women look up to and envy the life of one of world's most miserable women—Hillary Clinton. Women, once again, gave up everything and anything that gave them point and purpose in life, all for a masters degree (a stupid piece of paper), a commute, and a cold career in Corporate America which is dying by the day. A stock trader would deem that the worst kind of trade; buying at the top and selling at the bottom. Finally, there's Corporate America itself to blame.

The best thing for Corporate America was women entering the workforce. It lowered wages (increasing bottom line), it boosted demand for their products since women now had personal disposable income, and it created demand for a whole new list of products and services: Daycare facilities, additional cars, more gas, more insurance, more dining out, more cloths, more cell phones, more divorce lawyers, more child therapists, more crime, more hiring of police officers, more cleaning services, more Ritalin, more lithium/Xanax, more everything—the amount of material goods and services families have to buy now that you have two workers, no parents, and a need to outsource your child rearing easily boosted their sales by 50%. You must get it by now, don't you? You're a means to an end for Corporate America; as a consumer or employee you feed the same Master and that Master feeds you back a small portion.

It was a boon in terms of both sales and lower labour costs that only outsourcing to China would outdo. Of course, the family unit suffered greatly with divorce ravaging three generations, mal-raised children of broken homes drove up everybody's taxes, women were becoming less happy, and the country's finances went to shit, but it didn't matter. Women now had careers in Corporate America! And that's all that matters, right? Fuck everything else.

What do Men do now then?

It's a foregone conclusion that with the support of the government and corporations themselves, women will inexorably take over Corporate America. And any sober, realistic, self-respecting assessment of Corporate America will conclude we should let them have it. Men are smarter than to follow the herd or take on a dying horse into a race already half over. Women can't see the doom they are in or aren't willing to understand what deal they have with Corporate America—all they see is the "Rah-Rah you-go-gurl" cheerleaders on the side line and the appeal of finally having their name on a desk to show the "patriarchy" what a better slave they are to the machine. But, if men are going to give up Corporate America what are they supposed to do for work?

What do we do for employment? What do we do for our agency? What do we do in order to support ourselves and our lives to the fullest?

The prospective loss of what has traditionally kept us employed and alive is daunting, and willingly giving it up may seem insane. However, giving up on a career in Corporate America is a reality we're just going to have to face as there is no future there. Not only is it one we have to face, but one we should ultimately embrace. For while abandoning what has served as our primary means of support may be discouraging, we men have a trick up our sleeves that have served us well since time immemorial. We adapt.

Men have always adapted and women have always followed. Men are getting out of Corporate America just as women are entering because we know in our core that it is a dying horse. Understand Corporate America is a bubble waiting to be popped. It's the Titanic. It's going to run aground so you're better off living in reality and coming up with a Plan B or make sure you have a life raft at the ready to make your escape.

However, while many of you may not see an obvious alternative to Corporate America for employment, millions of men have already blazed the new trail and a much better form of employment—minimalism and entrepreneurship. Though not the traditional corporate career we originally wanted or were brought up to desire, minimalism and entrepreneurship is the only logical choice now for any man not already:

1. Steeped so far in Corporate America in terms of his career that it would not be economic for him to abort mission and start down the path of entrepreneurship, or

2. Indebted in terms of student loans, auto loans, mortgages, alimony, child support, etc., that he is a debt slave and therefore needs to be a corporate slave.

The reason why is that minimalism and entrepreneurship is indefinitely superior to working for a corporation. One, being a minimalist you do not need that much money to survive; especially as a man. You avoid debt easily; you avoid unnecessary expenditures and luxuries, and in doing so you not only minimize what you need, but maximize your freedom. This leads to a second important benefit—the ability to insist on employment standards.

If the pay isn't high enough, they won't let you telecommute, it isn't enjoyable work, or your client is just a fucking raging pimple dickhead, simple. You fire them. You just quit. You don't need the money and therefore can do without them. This also leads to a third major benefit—you can bluff your way to higher compensation. Unlike your divorced, debt-enslaved, Corporate American wage slave counterpart, you don't 'need' the money. You have a choice. You aren't a beggar, you're a chooser. This allows you to demand whatever you reasonably want per hour, because if you don't get it, so what? You don't NEED it. Alas, if done correctly, self-employment can, in the long run, become much more lucrative than a corporate slave career. Perhaps the single most important benefit of the minimalist-entrepreneurship lifestyle is the happiness (something people strive for in life) and sanity that comes with it. While you're sleeping in till 10am, your SuperPower-Tripping-Corporate-America-Power-Woman is waking up at 6am to suffer a commute. While you're at your local club or bar getting your morning coffee with Bailey's at 11 am to answer emails, your Rah-Rah empowered feminist counterpart is stuck in a boring meeting about setting up other meetings, begging the government for more grant money. When you decide you've done enough work for the day at 2pm and it's time to hit the gym or go hiking, your "You Go-Gurl" counterpart is only half way done with her day (not including her commute home). And when your kids come home from school at 4pm, you can take the out for fucking ice cream, go swimming with them, and give those noogies. The strong independent, divorced, Corporate America "Single Mom Hero" leaves her kids to decay in daycare all day long till 7pm; that's if traffic isn't a shit show.

It's simply a no-brainer. The sad tragedy, for women at least, is that men are one small epiphany away from switching our historic roles. It was already hard supporting oneself in the world. It's MUCH harder supporting a family now. But if socialist, sexist (and racist) political forces are going to insist on turning Corporate America into a childish insane asylum like today's Academia with "safe spaces," "mandatory diversity training," and blatant favoritism of women, forget it. I say it's time for a change.

Women fought so hard (as well as unfair and dirty) to get ahead in Corporate America, I cannot think of a better fate than to let them have it. And the only way to give it to them is to realize that losing Corporate America is no great loss, but a blessing. Let women do the work. Let women drive the commutes and suffer the Crab Basket at work now. Let women waste their lives in endless meetings about quarterlies and in cubes while the world passes them by.

I'm going fishing. I'm sleeping in. I'm working out. I'm going to do what I want. I'm just going to enjoy the decline. One of the questions that I asked you during the training was *why* **you** *are here.* This all was about me explaining to you how I did it and why I was doing the 9-5 grind. Now that we are at the end of the program it is time for you to start asking yourself seriously that very exact question. It's a difficult one and it's honestly the question you need to ask yourself before you start your actual tour of duty inside the real place: Corporate America. I truly believe now there are two types of people who come here to fight and partake in the War for a Paycheque: Those who *need* to and those who are here for the challenge, and the adventure. The guys who need to be here are the dudes who are either in debt or have a mortgage and wife to pay for (with kids as a side plate).

The real savages are what I call the 'contractors'; men who briefly enter the cubicle war for the quick money and then retire asap. There is no right way to fight in this climate, but the vast majority are not savages and are here in CorporateLand for the long haul; the 'contractors' making up the minority. I was a 'contractor' and don't regret it one bit and my training course that you've done through is tailored for both the long haulers and the 'contractors'. Now, why does CorporateLand need to churn our more long-haulers than the short burst hit men in suits? It's because America depends on the Beta male, without him our entire consumer economy would dive faster than a Russian sub in enemy waters.

The American Dream; sizeable suburban home, some land, a fence, two $30,000.00 cars, etc, which is romanticised to an extend that many Americans can't be satisfied with anything less as a long term goal. This is mainly why the War for a Paycheque will never end and will continue until everyone destroys each other. That, combined with the promotion of the rabid materialism, makes everyone susceptible to overspending in order to reach that goal, ensuring that they never have much to save; hence, perpetual servitude to cubicle life and to fight the good fight.

Of course, thanks to the promotion of the trope, most Americans still feel it is all worth it even if they *can't* afford it and go into debt. Then, you have another important trope involving work ethic. This stems from America's puritanical roots, and is an important reason why American in particular works more and vacation less than almost anyone in the developed world. This is the type of trope that keeps the average American cubicle grunt laboring almost constantly. All of these things, combined, help to ensure that the average American is always spending, never saving, and constantly producing for the corporate effort to churn out even more product for the consumer so that the good fight may continue. The wage-warrior, the majority of the USA populace, can't save and thus can't stop grinding it out in the cubicle warzone to defend this life.

Thus, you have a war, a game, in which there are no winners unless you make the game work for you. Majority of the people fighting at the office will lose because are fully invested in the game. They want the big house, the wife, the kids, the two or three cars and to hopefully get rich. The problem is, this isn't the 1950's battleground (The Golden Years) that your forefathers fought on. The war has changed and those very objectives listed above will now actually kill you financially in today's modern culture; the wife is now a liability sans new divorce laws and feminism.

There is no guarantee anymore that what you are fighting for will be there after you come home from the battle. So how has the battle changed and why are men still signing up for CorporateLand? The war, like I've said before, has changed. Men are now fighting a different battle in the cubicles. They are now starting to fight for themselves instead of fighting for the un-grateful (who were once grateful)—Being loyal to one's self is now the way to survive since the Home front is no longer what it used to be. The warriors that we are now churning out of CorporateLand will now become rouges and will be beholden to still serving America; but in a different way that will ultimately make it even stronger. A new brotherhood will be born and bred. You are now part of that brotherhood.

One final thought I would like to leave you with is that CorporateLand is like a game of chess when it all comes down to it. Even if you are a pawn and make it all the way to the other side and become a King, what have you gained, really? At the end of the day, when the sun goes down and the Game ends, all the pieces go back into the same box. How you play the Game is up to you, but just remember that.

Congrats, and Godspeed.

Made in the USA
San Bernardino, CA
13 January 2020